Praise for *Writing the Mind Alive* and Proprioceptive Writing®

"Proprioceptive Writing is shockingly, uncannily liberating. An enthralling, surprising journey into the self."

—STEPHEN LEVINE, M.D.
Professor of Psychiatry

"*Writing the Mind Alive* is the first writing book of the new millennium, and—in the tradition of Peter Elbow, Natalie Goldberg, and Anne Lamott—the next classic in the field. Metcalf and Simon's emphasis on hearing is a radically new contribution. Writers and educators, spiritual sojourners and psychotherapists—all will be inspired!"

—KAITLIN A. BRIGGS, ED.D.
Associate Director
Honors Writing and Thesis Research
University of Southern Maine

"The effect of Proprioceptive Writing on my work as an actor has been immeasurable. It has enabled me to finally find my voice and has given me a confidence I never believed possible. I am deeply indebted to the authors for this gift."

—D. W. MOFFETT
Stage, Screen, and Television actor

"I never thought I had a right to sing until PW showed my soul how to find its voice again."

—LINDA GOLDSTEIN
Singer and Grammy Award–Winning Music Producer

"If there was ever a process that could show you yourself in slow and compassionate doses, Proprioceptive Writing is it. I've relied on it for over eighteen years, and it's never let me down. This book is a true gift, the life's work of two master teachers. It puts Proprioceptive Writing in the palm of your hand."

—JANE BURDICK
Feldenkrais® Movement Teacher

"This book speaks with wisdom and lucidity. Anyone can profit from *Writing the Mind Alive*, a book elegant in its simplicity, persuasive in its intelligence, reassuring in its experience."

—VIVIAN GORNICK
Author of *Fierce Attachments*
and *The Situation and the Story*

"This book offers a unique writing approach that breaks right through writer's block, opens up inner treasures you didn't dream possible, and allows you to know yourself in an intimate, exciting way. It is beautifully executed, deeply inspiring, and psychologically on the mark."

—JILL MORRIS, PH.D.
Author of *The Dream Workbook*

"Proprioceptive Writing has helped me write, think, feel, and, most important, live more fully in the world and in myself."

—SUSAN GUTWILL
Psychotherapist
The Women's Therapy Centre Institute
Coauthor of *Eating Problems: A Feminist Psychoanalytic Treatment Model*

"This book is the Write Stuff. The excitement, wisdom, and practical guidance I gained from Linda and Toby in their workshop helped me connect with my creativity and complete a book for publication. Now all that is available in *Writing the Mind Alive*, and everyone can benefit from it."
—REV. DAVID JAMES RANDOLPH, PH.D.
Professor in Residence,
Graduate Theological Union, Berkeley, CA

"In *Writing the Mind Alive*, Metcalf and Simon set forth a method that promotes genuine clarity of thinking. It's practically like taking a bath in pen and words: wipe off enough grime, and you may be surprised how terrific you look. Proprioceptive Writing is the natural next step for fans of *The Artist's Way*."

—DREW MINTER
Singer and Stage Director

"Quite simply, this writing practice saved my life. At age fifty, the safety of the Proprioceptive Writing form led me gently back to heal the crippling grief of a motherless childhood and guided me though the chaos of breast cancer."

—GINNY KEEGAN
Real Estate Agent

"Proprioceptive Writing is a wisdom practice of the simplest and highest kind. It is a practice of liberation. One Write at a time."

—ANNE SHODO DELLENBAUGH
Zen Priest, Sheepscot River Refuge

"Every positive change I have been able to make in my life for the past ten years I owe to Proprioceptive Writing and the teaching of Linda Trichter Metcalf and Tobin Simon."
—NINA MORRIS-FARBER, PH.D.
New York City High School Teacher

"I have been practicing Proprioceptive Writing for fifteen years and will be eternally grateful for Linda's and Toby's work. It has helped me clarify my thinking and freed me to make important choices, in business and in my personal life."
—MAC McCABE
Entrepreneur and Management Consultant

"When I attended my first Proprioceptive Writing workshop, clutching my secret and terrifying desire to write, I could never have imagined what a gift Proprioceptive Writing would be for me. I've since published poetry and nonfiction, and I'm working on my second novel."
—ANNIE JACOBSEN
Pychotherapist, Teacher, and Writer

"In this exceptionally clear, cogent, and compelling book, Metcalf and Simon have made the remarkable practice of Proprioceptive Writing fully accessible to a wide public. While they make use of many of the techniques of psychotherapy, they have made a revolutionary advance by means of the Write, which provides a whole new dimension to the kind of reflection that goes on in talk therapy. Since reading the book, I have started doing the practice and have noted a definite jump in my reflective capacity and my general state of well-being."
—HOWARD KAMLER, PH.D., PSY.D.
Professor, Writer, and Research Psychoanalyst

Writing the Mind Alive

The Proprioceptive Method
for Finding Your Authentic Voice

LINDA TRICHTER METCALF, PH.D.,
AND TOBIN SIMON, PH.D.

BALLANTINE BOOKS
NEW YORK

A Ballantine Book
Published by The Random House Publishing Group
Copyright © 2002 by Linda Trichter Metcalf, Ph.D.,
and Tobin Simon, Ph.D.
Foreword copyright © 2002 by Christiane Northrup, M.D.

Grateful acknowledgment is made to New Directions Publishing Corp. and
Carcanet Press for permission to reprint "Danse Russe" from *Collected Poems:
1909–1939, Volume I*, copyright © 1938 by New Directions Publishing Corp.
Reprinted by permission of New Directions Publishing Corp.

www.ballantinebooks.com

Library of Congress Cataloging-in-Publication Data
Metcalf, Linda Trichter.
Writing the mind alive : the proprioceptive method for finding your
authentic voice / Linda Trichter Metcalf and Tobin Simon.— 1st ed.
p. cm.
Includes bibliographical references (p.).
1. English language—Rhetoric.   2. Report writing.
I. Simon, Tobin, 1941–   II. Title.
PE1408 .M48 2002
808'.042—dc21   2002025355

ISBN 0-345-43858-2

Cover design by Julie Metz
Cover photo © Louis B. Wallach, Inc./Image Bank

Text design by Holly Johnson

Manufactured in the United States of America

First Edition: June 2002

10   9   8   7   6   5   4   3

This book is dedicated to our students

Contents

Acknowledgments

To Alix Kates Shulman we owe our greatest thanks for the most fundamental, varied, openhearted help. Without her careful editorial assistance, this book would not be. What a gift from a writer!

We thank Christiane Northrup for taking time out of her busy schedule to write the foreword to this book. Her devotion to Proprioceptive Writing has been deeply gratifying.

We thank our agent, Sarah Jane Freymann, whose integrity compelled her to practice Proprioceptive Writing herself (to see if it worked) before she undertook to represent this book. Throughout the process of bringing it to publication, she has been an ally and guide. Thanks to Theresa Burns whose extensive publishing experience and considerable writing and organizational skills helped us make sometimes difficult thought available to a wide audience.

We thank Vivian Gornick, Annie Jacobsen, Patricia Reis, and Ann Snitow for reading an early draft of this manuscript, and for their sustaining support. We thank Jane Burdick and Sandra Deer for telling us what we needed to write when we'd completely forgotten. These and other dear friends kept our spirits up when they flagged. We thank every one of you.

We thank all the students who, over the years, have given us permission to use their Writes in teaching and in this book. A Write is a small moment in its author's life but says so much about all of us. To protect the privacy of the authors, we have changed their names and circumstances and have sometimes combined Writes. Still, we thank you for giving of yourself. We also thank Francis Trichter Metcalf for allowing us to make an example of him in this book and in our teaching. Lucky for us, such generosity is typical of him.

We are deeply indebted to those who have contributed their time, money, and professional services to the project of Proprioceptive Writing. Barbara Potter's friendship and support gave us the freedom to pursue our teaching goals. Our work could not have progressed without the generous help of Jane Burdick, Mary Bok, Jim Bowers, Kaitlin Briggs, Chên Sun Campbell, Jim Daniels, John Howard, Ben Levine, Stephen Levine, Mac McCabe, Charles Melcher, Bernie Meyers, Stephen Schneider, John Scholz, Peter Thompson, Scott York, and Rachel and Oscar Zurer. For this we are endlessly grateful.

Over the years many people have arranged workshops, provided teaching space, and spread the word about Proprioceptive Writing. We thank particularly Beverly Antaeus, Jocelyn Brando, Arifa Boehler, Anne Bright, Sue Carter, Marlee Coughlin, Mary Louise Cox, Sue Dunbar, Phyllis Frame, Phyllis Gerstein, Imogen Howe, Joan Lee Hunter, Ralph Hurwitz, Mary Johnston, Ginny Keegan, Peter Majoy, Polly Memhard, Alexandra Merrill, Nina Morris-Farber, Mark Mossie, Susan Muesse, Sharon Obeck, Karen Papadopoulos, Jennifer Polshek, Ira Rabois, Mia Simon, and Muff Worden. Special thanks to Susan Gutwill for introducing Proprioceptive Writing into the Renfrew community and for our collaborative teaching. We thank Melanie Wolf for collecting and editing documents on our behalf for the Institute for Noetic Sciences; to all who contributed letters and essays on Proprioceptive Writing, our heartfelt thanks. We thank Nancy Lunney of Esalen, Stephan Rechtschaffen of Omega, and Doug Wilson and Prue Berry of the Rowe Conference Center for their long-standing support of Proprioceptive Writing.

Thanks to the Threshold Foundation for their generous grant.

Jerome Trichter said to us early on, "Watch out or you'll get holy." We thank him for striking that cautionary note. He also observed, one evening at dinner, "This writing of yours is proprioceptive." We've never known whether to thank him or blame him for that comment.

We thank authors Oliver Sacks and Walter Ong for their writings, to which we have turned repeatedly to help us conceptualize proprioceptive failure and understand how hearing and writing influence consciousness. We thank Shirley Jackson for one helluva whodunit.

Finally, Toby thanks Linda for creating Proprioceptive Writing and Linda thanks Toby for grasping its value in a flash and for practicing it daily for twenty-five years. We want to thank each other for a quarter-century partnership in the development of Proprioceptive Writing, which has culminated in a seamless collaboration in writing this book.

Foreword

The essence of health is trusting yourself, your thoughts, and your feelings. Self-trust is the ability to know the truth about what you think and feel in your very bones—and then to use this information to guide your life.

But genuine self-trust is relatively uncommon in our culture. Instead, we are encouraged almost from birth to place our faith in the advice of authorities outside ourselves—schools, teachers, parents, and religious leaders, none of whom can possibly know our innermost thoughts and desires, the whisperings of our souls that are meant to inspire and guide us.

Without a way to check in with our deepest selves regularly, we gradually forget who and what we really are. We begin to develop an artificial persona whose actions and responses to life are driven by our desire to please others and meet their expectations.

I was thirty-two, pregnant with my second child, and pretty much living out of my efficient, medical-professional, steadfast, good-girl persona when I first met Linda and Toby at a Proprioceptive Writing workshop in Rockport, Maine. After having received an unsolicited brochure about Proprioceptive Writing in the mail, I had called Linda and asked her if this work could help me write about medical subjects more easily. She replied that whether one is a physicist writing a textbook or a novelist writing a story, the task is still the same: to find your writer's voice and express the essence of who you are and what you think in your writing.

This idea excited and energized me. It pointed to the possibility of *wholeness*—that somehow all of who I was and all of what I thought could be useful in my writing, even if I were addressing subjects like diabetes in pregnancy or the calcium requirements for breast-feeding mothers.

And so, in October of 1982, I sat down at a table with several others, lit a candle, listened to the music, took a breath, and began the process of listening to my thoughts and really turning in on them—feeling them in my body—as I asked the Proprioceptive Question, *"What do I mean by _____?"*

Over the next ten years, the miracle of Proprioceptive Writing and the combined (and separate) geniuses of Linda and Toby were the path I followed to reclaim my mind and my self-trust. Proprioceptive Writing was the map and the compass that guided me to the sure and steady experience of my own inner self. Proprioceptive Writing changed the way I think and listen to myself, and as a result it changed the way I heard others. The more I heard myself, the more energized my body became.

Linda had been correct. Through Proprioceptive Writing, I did indeed learn how to write about medical subjects more easily. But compared to reclaiming the fullness of my intellect, imagination, and intuition, that original goal seems pretty pallid! Proprioceptive Writing helped me forge the connections between my intellect, my heart, and my pen that eventually became the book *Women's Bodies, Women's Wisdom*, a work that I couldn't have dreamed possible in 1982, when I started Proprioceptive Writing.

So read this book. Light a candle. Put on your music. And begin the adventure of a lifetime—discovering the wonders of your mind and experiencing firsthand the fact that your thoughts have direction and a purpose you can trust. Feel how your thoughts connect with your emotions and your body in ways that surprise and delight you. Use this material to guide your life. Welcome to self-trust. Welcome to health.

—*Christiane Northrup, M.D.*

Introduction

The writing practice I discovered during the summer of 1976 was a revolution that shook me at my roots. Its effects astounded me: I began to know myself in new and startling ways. It opened me up, allowing me to feel things I could not feel before, to look at the world—and myself—with more compassionate eyes. Quite simply, it turned my life around, made each day fuller and more exciting.

That summer, through a simple writing method we now call Proprioceptive Writing, I reunited my heart and mind. For years, I'd been feeling alienated from myself: my intellectual thought and my emotions were isolated from each other; feelings drifted along their lonely course, unmodified by reason and reflection. This new kind of writing I was practicing seemed to bridge those divides, to make me feel vital and whole again. It helped me to think more feelingly and feel more thoughtfully. I had no theory then as to why this was so. But I knew it was crucial for me to continue writing in this way myself, and to teach others how to do the same. For the past twenty-five years that is what I have been doing, side by side with Toby Simon, my colleague and life partner.

Toby and I were professors of English and Humanities at Pratt Institute in New York when I first stumbled upon the writing practice that changed me that summer. After a few years of teaching Proprioceptive Writing in our classrooms and seeing the dramatic results it had on our students, we decided to leave academia, and in 1982 we founded the Proprioceptive Writing Center in Rockport, Maine. In 1987 we incorporated our center as a nonprofit educational institution and created a certified Proprioceptive Writing teachers' program. Over these many years we've taught our method to thousands of students—in groups and individually—at nearly a hundred venues. Our teachings have formed the basis of doctoral dissertations, have been the subject of studies at Harvard University's Graduate School of Education, and have been used in college psychology, education, and creativity programs. Proprioceptive Writing has been taught in the continuing education divisions of many colleges and secondary schools. In a modified form, it has been used to teach elementary-school children and home-schooled students from the first through fourth grades.

We know a lot more today about how Proprioceptive Writing works than we did in the late seventies. We've written this book to share with others what we've learned and the techniques we've taught our students in those thousands of sessions about this powerful approach to writing and self-knowledge.

How Does Proprioceptive Writing Work?

In Proprioceptive Writing we express our thoughts in writing so that we can reflect on them. It is a self-guided exercise that calls forth your imagination, your intellect, and your intuition all at once to open your heart and clear your mind. You practice it in twenty-five-minute sessions while listening to Baroque music, which roughly reflects the steady rhythm of the human pulse. At the end of each session you have produced a written work we call a Write.

As a ritual, Proprioceptive Writing has utter simplicity. People have compared its design to a Japanese garden or a mathematical formula. We sometimes describe it as a form to find meaning through feeling, to integrate emotion and intuition through language. Notwithstanding its simplicity, Proprioceptive Writing is profoundly deep, and can alter our lives in subtle and remarkable ways. It can be used as a path to self-expression and creativity, as a path to spiritual renewal, and as a path to emotional health. We do not use it to produce polished written works, though it may move us in that direction. Writing is not the end of the practice but rather the means to gain insight into and power over how we live and think. Although we may use it as a form of meditation or spiritual practice, it is not a religion.

Nor do we use it to diagnose psychological or emotional problems, though it may free us of some of their effects.

In the short term, Proprioceptive Writing invigorates our minds. Over time, it strengthens our sense of self and connects us to the world. When practiced regularly, Proprioceptive Writing can bring a new sense of well-being and confidence—absolutely vital to our mental health and creativity. It has an intense, slow burn and a long afterglow.

Unlike formal writing, Writes are neither good nor bad. They are not essays, prose poems, short stories, diary entries, or letters. Writes are never crafted, so no one assesses them for their art. They are not planned or polished. You never revise them. The magic that happens through a Proprioceptive Writing practice happens because of the feelings we uncover through our writing *while* we are completely focused on and attentive to our thoughts.

We sometimes wonder how anyone today can lead a fulfilling life without such a practice. Think of how often in your pressured, overscheduled life you are cut off from your own imagination and can't even hear yourself think, let alone sense the significance of what you're thinking. This failure to really listen to yourself, and to trust what you hear, is a roadblock to self-discovery and all the benefits that follow from it. It makes you feel isolated and numb, as I felt before that summer of 1976. Proprioceptive Writing can remove that roadblock, as it did for me, and put you on the path to health and self-trust.

While doing a Write, the first rule is to "write what you hear," to express on paper your immediate thoughts as if you were speaking them, communicating as directly as possible their tone and content. You try to get directly from the experience of a thought or feeling to the written expression of it, but this isn't always easy. Our minds, after all, are in motion all the time— thoughts appear and then slip away like balls of mercury as we chase them around the dark corners of our awareness. But with practice you learn to direct your hearing, to nudge your attention toward what is personally meaningful to you. Out of this focused listening comes detail, memory, story, revelation. You write it down, reflect on it, turn it this way and that, and, in doing so, come closer to knowing it. When we nourish our famished brains in this way, we feel a moment of uplift and expansion. The heart softens. The mind calms down. You feel more generous toward yourself and everyone else. There is no easy way to describe fully the sense of aliveness and pleasure that comes from expressing and reflecting on your thinking in this way, but over time you will come to understand it through the practice of Proprioceptive Writing.

MEDITATION OR THERAPY?

Many of our students see common elements between the practice of Proprioceptive Writing and meditation, and indeed there are similarities. Both require a regular, disciplined practice in a quiet environment, free of outer distraction. Both make use of certain props or aids that can deepen or mark off the practice. In meditation, we often use cushions or stools to set the spine straight, a candle to focus the eyes, incense to calm and please the senses. In Proprioceptive Writing, we keep a candle lit and play the slower movements of Baroque music during each twenty-five-minute session. The strongest common ground, however, is the focus on attention.

In Proprioceptive Writing, when the mind wanders, you wander with it on paper. When it becomes "stuck," or lands on a place you're curious about, you take notice and prod it with a mantralike question that asks what you mean by that thought. As with meditation, you try not to control your mind or force it into a direction; rather, you leave yourself open to discovery and surprise. Like meditation, Proprioceptive Writing can be practiced very effectively alone, but it can gain intensity and power if practiced in a group. Doing either requires very little preparation, equipment, or money.

The goal of both meditation and Proprioceptive Writing is to gain freedom from the attachment you have to your thoughts. The main difference between them is this: In our practice, you work toward this goal by *engaging* the thoughts and feelings that arise out of the exercise, while in meditation you seek to *let go* of them. Interestingly, some of our students are able to meditate only after developing a Proprioceptive Writing practice; they say it prepares the mind for meditation. Others find Proprioceptive Writing more satisfying than traditional meditation because it makes room for emotional expression. A minister who attended one of our workshops wrote to us soon afterward: "For me Proprioceptive Writing is the most productive kind of meditation I have used because it allows me to contemplate my feelings. Through my practice I have learned how letting go of control connects me to a higher power. A subtle paradox, yet very freeing. I am full of thanksgiving for this work."

For others, Proprioceptive Writing is most easily understood as a form of inner emotional work or therapy. As with psychotherapy, it generates insight and catharsis through close examination of subjective experience. But it also provides a framework for organizing this examination, eventually deepening the process, enabling us to use it to understand ourselves better, solve personal problems, and, ultimately, become happier. Interestingly enough, the first time we presented Proprioceptive Writing in a professional setting was not at a writer's workshop or even a teacher's training session, but to a group of psychiatrists at a midwestern medical school as part of a series on Innovative Therapies! Many of our students practice Proprioceptive Writing in conjunction with psychotherapy, often using their Writes to focus their therapy sessions. A film editor recently wrote to tell us that through Proprioceptive Writing she "got to places in my psyche that I've never tapped. . . . I have left many a shrink session wishing that the words and their articulateness hadn't gone into the ether, wishing they'd been recorded somewhere. Now I feel I have the access and the form at the same time—very exciting!" The fact that each session yields a written product was a bonus to her.

WHO CAN BENEFIT FROM PROPRIOCEPTIVE WRITING?

Proprioceptive Writing is easy to learn. The individuals and groups we've taught it to over the last two decades come from varied backgrounds and careers—from philosophers to business-people, from computer analysts to kids in junior high school—and all of them were able to grasp the basic technique in a very short time.

Despite our students' many differences, they all seem to share one thing: the sense that writing is profoundly linked to spiritual and mental health. We believe this proprioceptively—in our muscles and in our bones—and have made it the foundation of our teaching.

If you're a writer, or want to be one, Proprioceptive Writing can help you express yourself with greater authenticity and strength. It can help you focus your attention, develop discipline, and ameliorate performance anxiety. While it won't show you how to structure an essay, story, or poem, through a Proprioceptive Writing practice you'll learn to bring more honesty, more empathy, more of yourself into your work. Your writing will become more textured and fresh. In Chapter 3 we'll look much more closely at how individuals interested in formal or professional writing can benefit from the practice.

But beyond its effect on written expression, Proprioceptive Writing has profound effects on emotional life. Because the practice requires that you delve deep into the tender subjects that come up in Writes, you call up emotions, memories, and responses to situations from your past that have long been buried or ignored. Like a gardener digging up roots and rocks in the soil to make it healthier for new planting, when doing a Write, you're tilling the psyche, searching for clues to the person you are. Through Proprioceptive Writing you learn to narrate experience and, in the process, discover your life stories. You unburden the mind and resolve conflict. You experience episodes of heightened consciousness, an antidote to depression. The practice of Proprioceptive Writing fosters emotional health in myriad ways, promoting intimacy and spontaneity in personal relationships, the growth of emotional intelligence, and a sense of burgeoning creativity. We'll discuss more about the connection between Proprioceptive Writing and emotional health in Chapter 4.

People who have never experienced spiritual rewards can also benefit from Proprioceptive Writing. Given the pressures of life today, contemplative time is hard to come by for most of us. Even those who believe in the benefits of meditation and worship often have difficulty finding time in their busy, task-driven schedules for these practices. Writes can fill this gap. Not only does every Write have a psychological effect on the person writing it, but, as a record of one piece of the larger human experience, each Write contributes to the whole human story. A sense of the connection between your story and the larger whole, which develops through practice, is a spiritual experience. We'll look more closely at how Proprioceptive Writing can be used as a spiritual path in Chapter 5.

What are some of the other benefits of Proprioceptive Writing? They differ from person to person, of course, but most immediately our students report a sense of calm and an increase in energy level. (One of the first names suggested for the process was P.E.P., for Proprioceptive Exploratory Practice, because of the number of people who reported feeling "peppier" after doing it!) After some time, people usually notice an improved ability to focus and concentrate, a sharpness and clarity in their personal expression (both spoken *and* written), and an increase in spontaneity and self-confidence. Because, as we shall show, Proprioceptive Writing promotes self-understanding, regular practice deepens our capacity for empathy, the very foundation of all intimate relationships. Many of our students report that they read more and appreciate literature in a new way. Some say their dreams become lucid and detailed. Just about everyone reports feeling smarter and more creative. As with any exercise or discipline, the more you do it, the more dramatic the results tend to be.

Because it works so well as a tool of self-discovery, Proprioceptive Writing sometimes brings about changes in people's lives that they did not expect or feel prepared for; they may find themselves taking risks they had not had the courage or the capacity to take previously. One woman who had been divorced twice and had given up on men altogether fell in love; an engineer who hated his work left his well-paying job for a new, more satisfying but less certain career. Some take up a pursuit they never dreamed possible; others look up a friend or family member they haven't spoken to in years. We've often heard people describe the changes taking place in them as a kind of "homecoming."

A Word About Writing vs. Proprioceptive Writing

People who attend our workshops and private sessions include professional writers, would-be writers, former writers, and those who have never had any desire or ambition to write. We have taught scores of published writers, some quite well known. Experienced professionals like these find that regular practice dissolves inhibitions and cuts through writer's block. Here's how Camille, a playwright who's worked with us for years, puts it: "What Proprioceptive Writing allows me is a leap of imagination in the midst of intellect. By playing with the material of the intellect—words and meanings, ideas and memories—the raw ends get exposed, allowing new circuits to form and to connect. It is a perfect warm-up to my work on my formal writing projects."

Our many students who are not professional writers, but who hope some day to be one, come with their own ideas about what professional writing involves. Their individual relationships to the task of writing vary. Some struggle with it on a daily basis and never seem to get off the ground. Some write for the fun of it, for themselves or for friends and family, and wonder if they can reach a wider audience. Some were in love with writing at one time but stopped to focus on family, school, or career and now feel a strong desire to get back to it.

Yet even though an interest in writing is what brings them to us initially, many of these students soon become intrigued by the larger, less tangible benefits of Proprioceptive Writing. For them the practice becomes an end in itself.

We remember a student from several years ago, a travel agent from Miami who came to a workshop in New York. He burst into the room three hours late in his Hawaiian shirt and heavy gold chains expecting to be taught the tricks of the writing trade. We told him we did not help writers get published and we didn't teach craft—there are countless books already on the market that can help you if those are your specific goals. We told him that we had other valuable lessons to impart that could help his writing, so we encouraged him to settle down for the weekend—he'd made the trip, after all!—and learn about Proprioceptive Writing. In the end, though he did not get what he thought he had come for, he told us he got what he needed, and much more. He became a regular Proprioceptive Writing practitioner after that.

Although the Writes produced through Proprioceptive Writing often act as starter dough for a piece of publishable writing, we are always careful to distinguish between the two and urge our students to do the same. Proprioceptive Writing is an example of *private* or *process writing*—similar in some ways to psychologist Ira Progoff's system of keeping an "intensive journal" and to English professor and author Peter Elbow's popular "freewriting" method. Though both of these methods also involve getting past censors and increasing spontaneity in writing, Proprioceptive Writing involves inner listening and exploration of what one "hears" during a Write, and for this reason is considered more efficient by people who have tried all three methods. In fact, many of our workshop participants come to us because they feel they have dead-ended in one of these other forms and are looking for a process that goes deeper spiritually and emotionally. But any one of these methods is different from *public writing*—you would no sooner try to publish a Write or a piece of raw freewriting than you would present a live concert of musical scales.

Interestingly, many of our students whose careers have nothing to do with writing do eventually publish in their fields after practicing Proprioceptive Writing. Among them are several psychologists, ministers, and a physician, who have all attributed their later fluency to the practice.

But mostly our classes are filled with people who may have no ambition to publish, people perhaps much like yourselves—teachers, lawyers, therapists, school bus drivers, actors, housewives, stressed-out graduate students, editors, artists. Though we have on several occasions held workshops for specific groups—such as ministers or psychiatrists—our classes cut across class, gender, race, and age. Some of our students feel they have a novel in them or a book of poetry or a play. Others are seeking a fresh avenue for personal expression, confidence in their own authority, or simply a sense of their own voice.

How to Use This Book

Chapter 1, "The Sound of a Voice Thinking," portrays the discovery and evolution of Proprioceptive Writing. We'll introduce you to the mysterious "sixth sense" of proprioception and explain why we took its name for our method. Chapter 2, "Write What You Hear: How the Method Works," gives you all the information you need, step by step, to start a Proprioceptive Writing practice on your own at home, including all the materials you'll want to have on hand. This chapter discusses the frame of mind you need to adopt when approaching a Proprioceptive Writing session in order to reap the greatest benefits. We'll also answer the questions beginners frequently ask about the practice.

Chapters 3, 4, and 5 deal with the most useful applications of Proprioceptive Writing that our students have discovered over the last two decades. Chapter 3, "Self-Expression: The Method as a Path to Better Writing," explores how Proprioceptive Writing can be used as a path to formal writing and creativity. Though the development of our students' self-expression is most obvious in writing, the concepts in this chapter can easily be adapted to other forms of creative work—such as painting, dance, filmmaking, or photography. Chapter 4, "Proprioceptive Information: The Method as a Path to Emotional Health," will show how Proprioceptive Writing can help you discard useless or destructive ways of seeing and feeling, leading to greater flexibility and clarity. Chapter 5, "Awakening to Yourself: The Method as a Secular Spiritual Practice," discusses how

Proprioceptive Writing can become a discipline, much like daily meditation or prayer, helping to deepen your capacity for love. We strongly recommend that you read all three of these application chapters before you begin the practice. You'll learn a lot about how the method works by reading the examples and sample Writes of those who have practiced Proprioceptive Writing.

In Chapter 6, "Creating a Lifelong Practice," we'll share with you ways of enriching your individual practice and incorporating it into your life. We'll give you suggestions for starting a Proprioceptive Writing group of your own, for doing Writes with your partner or children, and for organizing your Writes so that they may be useful to you in the future. Some people fall in love with their Writes. Some store them in special folders and refer to them when they feel the need. One of our students, a nature photographer, bound his Writes beautifully in book form.

As we often tell students, the basic techniques of Proprioceptive Writing can be taught. But the breakthroughs and discoveries it leads to depend on the work you do with it, day after day, week after week. The more frequently and attentively you do Proprioceptive Writing, the more dramatically you will feel its effects. We can start you off, but only you can make the practice an integral and necessary part of your life. When you do, you will find that there is no limit to your mind's ability to engage and surprise you, no bottom to the depth of your capacity for feeling. The following words are from a former student, not a minister or psychologist or artist but a stockbroker who was feeling "lost" in mid-life:

You reintroduced me to the poet inside me and she, in turn, has introduced me to many of her voices: the lover, the linguist, the scholar, the analyst, the athlete, the musician, the actress, the comic, the cynic, the teacher, the student, the philosopher, the parent, the censor, the smart-ass. I found the writer inside and she led me back to my husband, my children, my parents, friends and acquaintances, my house and my home town, my past and present, as well as my God and my values. I want to thank you and Proprioceptive Writing for the confidence you have given me. I am calmer and delight more in the present. I think I am becoming the kind of person I have always imagined I could be.

L.T.M.

Writing the Mind Alive

Chapter One

The Sound
of a Voice Thinking

The self-explorer, whether he wants to or not,
becomes the explorer of everything else.
—ELIAS CANETTI

It was Ralph Waldo Emerson who said, "Trust thyself: every heart vibrates to that iron string." In the one hundred and fifty years since he issued his once radical decree, self-trust, in the guise of "self-esteem" and "self-confidence," has become a commonplace goal. But that trust is still elusive for most of us. Despite our openness to self-exploration, efforts to acquire it often fail.

Yet so much of what is worthwhile in life is grounded in self-trust: relationships, finding the right work, your ability to learn and create, your willingness to take risks, connection with your desires and your ideals. Self-trust allows you to appreciate the quality of your own mind as well as the minds of others. Through self-trust you gain the gift of yourself.

By self-trust we mean having an intimate feel for the person you are and the way your mind works. Imagine visiting the country of You and becoming comfortable with its language, its customs and idiosyncrasies, the contours of its landscapes, its unique history. Imagine discovering what it's like to be you, how it feels to be in your skin, to think your thoughts, to possess your memories, to be shaped by your stories, to be driven by your obsessions, to be happy or unhappy as only you are, to perceive yourself and others as only you do. Self-trust begins with an honest exploration of your thoughts and feelings, which are as close to you as the food you eat and the air you breathe.

Sadly, many people are too fearful, anxious, or rushed for such intimate self-exploration. They feel disconnected from their subjective experience. This condition leaves them in a state not of self-trust but of self-doubt. In fact, it was an agonizing state of self-doubt—a feeling of being completely cut off from her own inner life—that more than twenty-five years ago led Linda to create Proprioceptive Writing.

How It All Started: Linda's Story

If necessity is the mother of invention, it was need that forced me to invent Proprioceptive Writing. Soon after my mother died, when I was seven, I had started feeling as if I were locked inside myself and couldn't get out, or locked outside and couldn't get in. Psychologically, I was suffering from what I now call proprioceptive deficit, a breakdown in communication between a person and his or her subjective thoughts. By some strange act of compartmentalization, I kept my private thoughts secret from myself and so felt cut off from them. Most days, this condition was my prison.

A year after he was widowed, my father remarried. The tension among my father, stepmother, older sister, and myself seemed to me an unchanging aspect of life, like a gloomy weather system that blows in and won't blow out. During certain moments, however, I would feel a brief reprieve.

Before I fell asleep some nights, I entered a state of mind that compensated for all my daytime hardship and taught me how to live with it. As I lay in bed, reviewing the past day or planning new escapes, something clicked inside my head that altered my perspective on myself in a startling way. With my inner eye I pictured my thoughts; with my inner ear I heard myself speaking them, and suddenly I knew myself as a thinker thinking. "I think, therefore I am," as Descartes famously said. This spontaneous awareness brought with it a feeling of harmony and love. Contentment washed over me at those times.

Everyone has experiences of heightened consciousness; they come unbidden. Mine taught me two of life's great lessons: that as thinker I had power, and that the thinking process could be my pleasure. But this pleasure was mercurial. It came and went. Sometimes I'd lie awake for hours, waiting for that special feeling to kick in, and nothing would happen.

The first time I became aware of how cut off I was from myself I was eleven, and all the other kids at summer camp were writing in journals. "Dear Diary," my friend Karen wrote blithely, lying on her belly in the bunk bed below and kicking her legs in the air. "Today we went on a hard hike up Mount Kildare and Andy kissed me but no one saw us. He's the best boy in the group. Maybe I love him. I'm not saying yes." I hung over the side of our double-decker, watching Karen write, and felt a stab of emptiness. Not three feet from me, she was lost in her imagination. Some kids gave their diaries names, like Louisa or Amy or Rebecca, but we all knew that when you wrote in a diary you were your own audience. Who was this alter ego to whom Karen spoke her thoughts for the pleasure of it? I hadn't a clue how to have the kind of imaginative presence to myself that my friend had that day.

Years later, when I was a college student writing papers, a moment sometimes came (rarely, but remarkably) when my thoughts absorbed me totally, and I felt engaged, both emotionally and intellectually. A warmth suffused me in that instant. I felt that universal love and personal well-being I had known as a young girl thinking in my bed. But more usually my mind felt impenetrable to me. I wanted to reflect on my thinking, carefully and deeply, but writing with the purpose of self-discovery was an alien concept then. We were encouraged to analyze, that was all. However competently I could dissect a writer's thoughts, I could not narrate my own.

How could I free my mind and become available to what actually interested me? How could I recognize desire, move on impulse, develop will? How could I exert myself on my behalf? How could I be less afraid of difficulty and choose the thing that was harder but more personally rewarding for me? Where to begin? The answers came during the summer of 1976, when the doors to my consciousness opened and the distinction between inside and outside dissolved.

I'd been teaching English literature at Pratt Institute in Brooklyn for six years and needed to write my Ph.D. dissertation to stay on a tenure track. While I was looking through my card file of authors on whom I wanted to do research, I came across a book that had struck me as extraordinary when I'd read it several years earlier. *We Have Always Lived in the Castle* is a short novel by Shirley Jackson, best known as the author of "The Lottery," a short story originally published in *The New Yorker* in 1948 and frequently anthologized since then. The book is a psychological portrait of a young girl named Mary Katherine in mid-twentieth-century New England, a brilliant depiction of female terror and subverted aggression, but also a spoof of a traditional whodunit. In this case, Mary Katherine had done what many young girls only fantasize about: laced sugar with cyanide and eliminated mother, father, an annoying younger brother, and a useless aunt, all in the time it takes to drink your after-dinner coffee. Thereafter, she remains in the decaying family estate, behind tall wrought-iron gates, along with her adored older sister. With nothing more to do than light dusting once a week, she has all the time in the world to dwell on her thoughts.

Reading the book over again brought back the sound of Mary Katherine's voice, which had struck me when I first read it and stayed with me over the years. The novel is written entirely as Mary Katherine's internal dramatic monologue. Throughout the book she is holding a silent, one-way conversation with her chief admirer: herself. To this self she speaks her thoughts in the order that they come to her, making side remarks for her amusement, rehearsing insults she'll deliver, loving whom she loves, hating whom she hates, recalling as if for the first time what she's said a thousand times before. No one notices her deceptions or self-delusions—except, of course, the reader. She's safe in her seclusion, free to travel where her thoughts take her, obsessing to her heart's content.

This thinking voice sounded amazingly alive to me. Jackson had found a narrative voice—it was *the sound of a voice thinking*. I repeated the phrase to myself; it was like a koan or a riddle. Back then I felt so cut off from myself that I'd forgotten the connection between silent inner thought and spoken thought that every child takes for granted and that Jackson had captured so deftly. There was something here I needed to understand. My goal, my obsession that summer, was to learn how Jackson made that connection and captured that sound for her narrative voice. It didn't occur to me at the time that I might find my own thinking voice in the process.

It was early June when I lit a candle and flipped on a tape of Bach cantatas—just an inspiration to support the morning's work. I opened the novel and began to read Mary Katherine's "uncensored" thought. Her voice came in loud and clear. Taking my cue from her, I wrote down my every thought, without letup. I interacted with Mary Katherine, reacted to her, advocated for her, and, in my fashion, imitated her as well. When my thoughts wandered away from Jackson's text to my life or emotions, I wandered with them. Without a reason to edit my thoughts, I elaborated on them all, exploring in a leisurely fashion every psychological event aroused in my mind by my sense of the words I was using. Three hours later I awakened to the room I was in and looked around. I turned off the music and blew out the candle. I felt uncommon calm. I had lost myself in time, but never had I felt as much myself. Something wonderful was happening to me and it took place through this writing: I was writing solely for myself while addressing a listener who shared the same sense of the subject as I did. For the first time in my life I was following my thoughts wherever they led me, no matter what the terrain. I was entering into my own life by exploring my own thought flow.

Mary Katherine's every thought contained a story. Her words were charged with feeling. Her tones were fluid: bitter, haughty, ironic, evasive, fearful. She took for granted her right to think her inner thoughts out loud, obsessive and emotion-driven as they were.

Jackson had brought powerful attention to her task as writer and I took permission from her to equal that attention and turn it toward myself, to listen to my words as they spilled onto the paper, sense the feelings and motives they concealed, and amplify them. Soon enough, I was writing my own stories of experience, amazed to find I had them in me.

And so I worked, six hours each day, five days a week, for the next three months. The only sound I heard was Baroque music and the dripping of the wax. By the end of the summer, I'd become a student of my own life. Just as I had come to know Mary Katherine through the stories she told about her life and the shifting tones in which she told them, so I came to know myself through my own stories and the voice that told them.

Could I have had this breakthrough without writing? I'm certain I couldn't have. Before that summer I couldn't express my feelings or understand my subjective experience. Only when I began to speak with myself, while a script rolled out from beneath my pen, did my inner thoughts become a voice that I could hear. It was as if that voice was a fictional persona and another part of me sat back and listened to it. Through writing I was creating a space between me and my thinking. Just as a narrator or character is of an author but not the author (no more than Iago is Shakespeare), so my thoughts and feelings were of me but not me. Like an author whose consciousness is larger than the fiction she creates, I found within myself a consciousness greater than the personal experiences I recorded.

To identify with the thinker within yourself rather than with the thoughts you are thinking is like finding you have a lover by your side. Revelations come tumbling in and with them a sense of spaciousness and grace. Not since I was a child of eight, lying in my bed, dreaming my waking thoughts, had I felt such peace. The slant of light through which the world entered me widened: by gaining entry into my own consciousness I had found the means of entering the life and consciousness of others.

As the end of summer approached, I began to think about

my fall classes and the students I'd soon be teaching. I decided to bring my new writing practice to Pratt. I would lead my students by instruction, step by step, day by day, and by example. I vowed to hear them in their writing as I had heard myself in mine, and to show them, in turn, how to listen to themselves in a new way. Using the rules I had developed, they wouldn't need six hours of daily writing for three months to get them going, as I had needed. One half hour, when done right, would do just fine.

But first, I wanted to be able to explain why this new kind of writing worked—and what to call it. Luckily, a little-known system discovered in the nineteenth century gave me the answers to both of my questions.

Why Such a Funny Name?

What is "proprioception"? As children we played a little game. Palms upward, fingers knit together, we'd wiggle the finger a friend pointed to but did not touch. That we could move the finger at all amused us. We hesitated before we located it. How did we find the right one? We sensed *within ourselves* where it was.

The word *proprioception*, which comes from the Latin *proprius*, meaning "one's own," normally refers to our body's proprioceptive system. Just as the five senses take in information about the *outer* world—what we see, touch, smell, taste, and hear—and transmit it to our brains, the little-known "sixth sense" of proprioception also gathers and processes information, but from the inner world of our bodies, the world we alone inhabit.

Within this system, actual nerves, called proprioceptors, located in the muscles, joints, and tendons communicate back and forth with the brain, orienting the body to its own movement, position, and tone. So that when we walk, we know where our legs are, and our legs know where we want to move. We can grasp a flower or a glass of water without crushing or dropping it. It's because of our proprioceptive sense that we know how to raise and lower our arm without looking at it, that our facial muscles know how to smile, that our hand can locate an itchy nose in need of scratching—automatically and without stopping to think.

Through proprioception, we are also able to synthesize emotion and imagination. When we watch a bird in flight, for instance, and "feel" in ourselves, in our muscles and our bones, the uplift, glide, and soaring movement of that bird . . . that feeling is a proprioceptive one. When we dance to music without knowing steps, or sing a song without knowing notes, those musical feelings are proprioceptive, too. We can dance and sing *by feel*. For this reason the proprioceptive system may be viewed as the interface of body and mind, as well as the source of emotional expression: by virtue of proprioception, we react to what we see, hear, smell, touch, taste, *and feel*—bodily, as well as mentally.

Nobel laureate and pioneering neurophysiologist Sir Charles Scott Sherrington first identified the system a little over a hundred years ago. According to esteemed British writer and neurologist Oliver Sacks, Sherrington named it proprioception "because of its indispensability for our sense of *ourselves*; for it is only by courtesy of proprioception . . . that we feel our bodies as proper to us, as our 'property,' as our own." If our proprioceptive system were to become damaged through accident or illness, we would lose the feeling of embodiment, our *us-ness*, that we take for granted when in health.

In an essay entitled "The Disembodied Lady," from his best-selling book *The Man Who Mistook His Wife for a Hat*, Sacks describes the devastating effects of proprioceptive loss afflicting one of his patients, Christina. Because of a virus that attacked her proprioceptive nerve fibers, Christina's sensory control loops had broken down. On a physical level, described Sacks, her body lost all sense of position and tone. She could not move, sit, or stand—and whenever she tried to, her entire body collapsed. We have language to describe what it feels like to live without sight, sound, touch, taste, or smell. But as Sacks says, no language exists to describe what it feels like to live without a proprioceptive sense of our own bodies. When asked to describe how she felt, Christina borrowed the language of emotional trauma: she felt empty and unreal, pithed, disembodied, inauthentic.

When we call our method Proprioceptive Writing, we are using the term metaphorically, comparing the mind's capacity to know itself to the body's. Through the transmission of proprioceptive information, the body has an ongoing sense of its own identity. In a similar way, the mind is also proprioceptive;

it "knows" itself whenever we become aware of our own perceptions and feel their meaning to us. It is precisely the mind's need for this kind of subjective information that Proprioceptive Writing satisfies. Although initially we called our practice the Thinking-Writing Method, the metaphor of proprioception seemed so illuminating as a model that we changed our name to reflect it.

Sacks's story brought the proprioceptive system to the attention of contemporary readers. But at least a decade earlier the proprioceptive sense was in the air and references to it turned up in the unpublished writings of the American poet Charles Olson. Olson, like Ezra Pound and T. S. Eliot, believed that poetry, by transforming consciousness, could revitalize Western civilization. In his prose poem "Proprioception," he uses proprioception as metaphor and symbol for the unification of the mind/body split, even claiming: "the soul is proprioceptive."

But the usage of the term that comes closest to our own is the one David Bohm invokes in his work *On Dialogue*. A protégé of Einstein and an important twentieth-century physicist, Bohm was concerned with how thought, feeling, and memory—in other words, consciousness—shape our reality. He believed that "the proprioception of thought," by which he meant "thought aware of itself in action," could change consciousness if we listen to ourselves and others openly. We believe the method we began teaching in the late seventies, and subsequently called Proprioceptive Writing, has the potential to make the change in consciousness Bohm envisioned. To understand how, we need to first explain what actually goes on during a

Write—how exactly we transform our thinking into voice on the page.

Putting Voice Back into Writing

People who attend our workshops bring with them a lot of old baggage about writing. A school-learned task for most, writing was often used as a measure of success or failure, like a test. To sweep away these associations, we sometimes begin a workshop by recontextualizing the act of writing, presenting it for what it is most fundamentally: a technology for storing speech sounds.

Before the invention of writing, the human voice was the only instrument for conveying thought and recording facts. With the invention of writing our way of remembering changed. Using alphabet-based writing, people recorded their thoughts by preserving the sounds of words in combinations of graphic symbols called letters. (Some written languages, like ancient Egyptian hieroglyphics, Chinese, and Native American scripts, developed from pictographs and ideographs but also have a strong sound component.) Little about this basic process has changed to this day: the use of writing to record sound, whether done by hand, computer, or other instrument, preserves thoughts and anything expressed by words, including feelings, observations, and information, such as when wars take place, where people are born and die, and what things cost.

Although we take it for granted now, the introduction of a technology that transcribes the sounds of speech was an astounding invention—on a par with the harnessing of fire, an event that changed forever the relationship humans had to the world. Not long ago we watched a television documentary about the destruction of virgin rain forest in Brazil, in which indigenous people with an oral tradition confronted a written text for the first time in their lives. Two literate men from a first-world country sat in a circle and introduced a little game to the people of the forest. One man, clad in Bermuda shorts, says to the bare-limbed fellow by his side: "Whisper a message in my ear." The bare-limbed man does so, and the man in Bermuda shorts writes it down on a pad, then passes the pad around the circle until it reaches his literate partner on the other side of the room, who reads the message aloud.

The oral folk stare at the paper confused and amazed. On it they see some scraggly lines, some curves and dots, but nothing that transmits information or meaning to them. They pass the pad back and forth. They turn it over. They shake it. They throw it on the ground and lift it up again, press their ears against it, consult each other in hushed and nervous tones: "Can you hear the pad?" they ask. "Does it speak to you?" Each takes a turn listening but the pad does not speak. Why, then, will it speak to the literates? What power do they possess that activates voice without the use of sound? Nothing in nature explains what the forest people have heard and witnessed in the circle.

As the reaction of these oral folk dramatizes, the impact writing has on the psyche represents a new separation of the previously indivisible mind/body unit. This is the subject of

Orality and Literacy, a remarkable work by Walter J. Ong, S.J., internationally renowned scholar, teacher, and writer, who has written extensively on the shaping influence of the alphabet, writing, and print on human consciousness. As Ong explains, writing removes thought from its natural habitat in sound and locks it permanently into a visual field forever.

Consider this simple illustration. Imagine sending your neighbor a note with these words on it: "Come over for dinner tomorrow night." From the written words alone, the neighbor can't tell what would be perfectly obvious if the words had been spoken in person—when the invitation was made, by whom, for what evening, in what tone and spirit. When uttered by a speaker, much meaning can be derived from context. By contrast, writing separates and extends voice *away* from the speaker. Writing nails down on paper the words of the person speaking—*but just the words*. Everything else that pertains to those words, what the actual context communicates, the written message leaves out.

When you write your thoughts in Proprioceptive Writing, you bring to the visual presence of writing the aural presence of speech. We ask you to think of your thoughts in a radically new way (though it's really an ancient way as well). We ask you to imagine giving thought voice as you think it. This is easier than it sounds once you get the knack of it. You just pretend to be speaking on paper. You can always find words for anything in your mind: your ideas, feelings, mental images, beliefs, opinions, doubts, questions, reasons, memories, hopes, fantasies, regrets, disappointments, suppositions, fears, longings, desires, confusions. Every form of thought you can turn into words in your Writes. In Proprioceptive Writing, voice becomes the organ of thought and every human being has his or her own.

Awakening the Auditory Imagination

When you make the shift in Proprioceptive Writing from experiencing thought as mere words in your head to a living voice in your ear, your relationship to your thinking changes. You begin to awaken what T. S. Eliot called "auditory inwardness" and what in Proprioceptive Writing we call the *auditory imagination*—the capacity to enter your thoughts in an interested, nonjudgmental way and gain awareness of yourself from them. In terms of your psychological and spiritual well-being, this capacity is one of the most valuable you'll ever develop.

As we saw in the last section, the first step in finding your voice through Proprioceptive Writing is capturing your actual moment-to-moment thoughts in writing. The second, equally important, part is *overhearing* them *as if they were spoken*. Everyone has the innate capacity to do both; what we "say" we can "hear." So why not make full use of that capacity? After all, if we do not hear our own thoughts and gain information from them, we might as well be thinking someone else's. If you practice Proprioceptive Writing, you'll develop an awareness of the sound of your thinking. You'll begin to imagine your thoughts as a persona with a voice.

People often report to us that though a particular story they tell in a Write may be one they've told before, perhaps to their therapists, they have a more complete emotional experience of it in their Writes. Because they hear their thoughts differently *as* they are writing them, they imagine them more fully. And what they imagine most fully, they care most about.

The kind of hearing we do during a Write requires our total and undivided attention. To get a sense of what this attention feels like, imagine for a minute watching a movie about a double agent on the run. To lose himself in a crowd, our hero crashes an elegant cocktail party. We see him in the middle of the screen trying to blend in; we hear the clinking of glasses and the murmur of the guests all around him. Suddenly, the agent remembers an earlier conversation that hinted at the danger in which he now finds himself. To indicate to the audience that the character has withdrawn his awareness from the surrounding crowd and is focused totally on replaying that conversation in his head, the director cuts the sound of everything else. We see the moving mouths of the animated faces in the room but we no longer hear their voices. All we hear is our hero's thoughts—remembering that conversation, realizing its importance, sensing his current danger, plotting his next move. For us in the audience it's like an intense form of eavesdropping. To overhear ourselves in Proprioceptive Writing, we must give our total attention to the sounds of our thoughts. Like our hero, we cannot hear ourselves think and listen to anything else at the same time.

Not Just Expressing but Reflecting

From time to time a student asks: If overhearing our thoughts as if they were voiced is so crucial to Proprioceptive Writing, why write down anything at all? Why not just speak our thoughts and focus on hearing them? Because by slowing thought down to the time it takes to write it, and by holding thought still, we can *reflect on* our thoughts.

Expression isn't enough; reflection is also required. Reflection is what makes Proprioceptive Writing different from automatic writing, free writing, morning pages, stream of consciousness, or any form of process writing that separates expression from reflection, encourages expression over reflection, or views thinking as a distraction. We view thinking as an act of imagination and reflection an inquiry into that act. In Proprioceptive Writing, reflection is a spontaneous response to whatever feeling or idea you are expressing, the other end of the seesaw. It's a natural gesture that allows you to elaborate your thoughts and examine their meaning in the light of emotion and reason.

Writing supports your reflections because it holds thoughts still. A disappearing target like spoken thought is not good for reflection, but written thought stays put. When people ask us if they can do Proprioceptive Writing without writing—say, by thinking out loud into a tape recorder—we tell them no. You're expressing your thoughts in writing so you can reflect on them.

When you gain new information from your reflections, like the double agent in the movie, you make adjustments. Your point of view shifts. Your perspective deepens. Your personal intelligence expands. In this mental movement you sense your vitality. All the metaphors we've heard people use to convey the effect of Proprioceptive Writing on a sheer feeling level are ones of movement: expansion, uplift, transport, being born into or thrust into, in the flow, in the zone—and all follow from your ability to reflect imaginatively on your own thinking.

A New Kind of Teaching

We had arrived at Pratt around the same time in the late 1960s to teach in the Department of English and Humanities. We both planned to stay on the track toward tenured professorship, but everything changed when Linda began teaching Proprioceptive Writing in the fall of 1976. Soon after, she introduced the process to Toby, who became an enthusiastic practitioner and teacher. Together and separately we taught graduate students, remedial writing students, advanced placement students, and students in our humanities and literature courses. It was also around that time that we became life partners.

The effects of Proprioceptive Writing on our students was dramatic. Their motivation for learning intensified. Their concentration deepened. Their ability to express complex thoughts in writing and speech grew stronger. They relaxed, becoming more generous in their responses to one another and more open about themselves. Our classrooms became scenes of learning explosions.

We held Proprioceptive Writing tutorials with fine arts graduate students who were struggling to write their master's theses. Soon, they were producing essays on their work that not only developed their confidence but also brought us highly encouraging feedback from their art and architecture teachers who came to us to talk about the changes they were noticing in the work of undergrads whom we shared. The more adept these students became at expressing their ideas and reflecting on them in writing, the more personal and revealing their art became. As one said in a note we still have, "By learning to address important questions in my writing, I've opened up whole areas to be explored visually. Getting to know my own thinking has made clear the direction my artwork should take. Becoming a focused thinker has made me a more honest artist."

In our content courses (literature, women's studies, oriental culture, mythology), as well, students were writing their minds alive, integrating ideas into their writing with an ease we hadn't seen before. As their hearing of themselves sharpened, they became markedly better readers and appreciated literature in a new way, too. At a time when many college-aged kids were experimenting with drugs, our students were getting a natural high from their Proprioceptive Writing sessions.

We knew we'd developed a practice that, when done regularly, could be transformational. It had altered our work and enriched our lives. We'd found a calling. In the spring of 1978, we made the difficult but important decision to give up our tenure-track positions at Pratt and devote ourselves full-time to teaching Proprioceptive Writing. Twenty-five years later, it's still our life's work.

We remember many of our students from that time, of course, but one young man in particular stands out. Jesse was in the very first Proprioceptive Writing class Linda taught at Pratt and he continued to work with us for the next several years. In his senior year, Jesse developed a brain tumor and had to leave school shortly before graduation, but he continued his practice, and after we moved to Maine his parents drove him up from New York to work with us privately. A month after our last series of Writes together, his parents informed us of Jesse's death. They told us how much the process had meant to their son, how it helped him believe in himself during the years of his illness, and kept his spirit alive. When Jesse was doing his Writes, they explained, he was a happier person.

All human beings think, in the ordinary sense, but not everyone takes pleasure in reflecting on their inner thoughts. Such heightened consciousness is what Proprioceptive Writing develops. In the next chapter we'll teach you how to begin.

Chapter Two

Write What You Hear:
How the Method Works

---

*The true beginning of wisdom is the desire of
discipline, and the care of discipline is love.*
—THE WISDOM OF SOLOMON, 6:17

While some beginners say that Proprioceptive Writing has too
many rules and too much structure, others worry that it has
too few rules, that there's nothing to hold on to. Every new
practice seems mysterious. Think of the first time you did yoga,
or meditated, or were caught up in a courtship. Though at
first the process may seem unfathomable, the rewards come
eventually.

Take advantage of the structure of Proprioceptive Writing.
Follow the simple instructions we give you in this chapter, and
start your practice. As Toby often says, all firsts are awkward . . .
but awesome. The deeper you sink into the form, the more
natural and necessary it will seem.

STARTING THE WORKSHOP

On the morning a new workshop starts, we always wake up early. No matter how many years we have been teaching, there is something stirring about that first session—the very air seems charged with possibility. Whether we're on the road or teaching at our own center, the night before we put time and care into setting up our work space. Over the years we've had many different offices, but the writing room is always similar: sparsely furnished and almost entirely free of decoration, calm and quiet—more like a temple or a zendo than a place to socialize. Several long wooden tables line the walls. In the center of the room are two comfortable couches, one or two easy chairs, and a handful of colorful cushions in a circle where people sit when not writing. We try to create an inviting space where participants can feel honored, safe—even loved.

We enjoy watching students as they first come in, smile a little tentatively at the others, and find seats in the circle. Most take their shoes off without our asking. After the last person has arrived and is seated, it seems that all at once the small talk dies down and a hush settles on the group—our cue that they are ready to begin.

Some of those present are new to Proprioceptive Writing. Others are seasoned practitioners. We prefer to avoid formal introductions and have never standardized our opening remarks. What we want to do is establish our context for being together and begin the work of thinking in writing. Sometimes we ask people to write down their reasons for attending the workshop:

I'm a journalist and would-be memoirist and have taken years of writing classes. I'm very well versed in what you might call the "confessional writing workshop." But I'm feeling a strong sense of inhibition lately in both my professional and personal writing, and I need something new to help me push past it.

I used to write a lot years ago and always enjoyed it—I kept a journal for twenty years. Now I want to go deeper in my writing, not just report the events of the day, but get at something larger.

My psychotherapist recommended this workshop. She took it herself and thought I would like it. I'm a pretty creative person, but years of working in the business environment have dulled my edges.

Sometimes we ask participants to make a wish in writing: If this workshop could give you what you most want, what would that be? If someone says, "I want to come up with an outline for my first novel," we can clarify the differences between our work and traditional writing workshops. But mostly what they seem to want is a new way of writing or a new way of thinking that can help them meet the challenges in their life.

What I want more than anything else in the world right now is the feeling that I'm moving in the right direction.

I have a strong desire to paint, to be an artist. But I never get to that place. I need a systematic, disciplined approach to find out what I want to say in my art, so I can settle down and take myself seriously.

Sometimes a participant asks a question right off the bat that serves as our introduction. More often, we ask questions that reflect on our subject indirectly: Isn't it odd, we might ask, that you can not *know* yourself? That you can have experience without knowing it? That you can think without hearing yourself think? That you can have feelings you're not aware of? Sometimes we begin by discussing the distinction between process writing, of which Proprioceptive Writing is an example, and formal writing, or writing intended for a reading public.

When we sense that the group is beginning to think along with us, we turn to the heart of the matter. Briefly and concretely, we tell them how to practice Proprioceptive Writing. We give the essentials. We know that after they have been writing awhile, the process will become clear. We answer a few of their questions, promising to answer more later. Then we invite them to the table.

It's an intense moment—everyone feels it. The quiet of the room is deep. The seriousness of the participants is palpable. They rise and make their way across the room slowly and choose their places. We light the candles. As the music starts and they take up their pens, the atmosphere is as electric as it was in the first workshop we held, more than twenty-five years ago. This moment, this beginning, is a new beginning—and we feel joy and gratitude in it.

PRACTICING ON YOUR OWN

First, you need to get comfortable being alone with yourself. You need to create a sense of solitude. Solitude is less a physical condition than a state of mind in which you can be yourself, whoever you are. You can set yourself up in a room alone, write in a journal, or do morning pages, and still live uncomfortably with judgment figures in your head. If you have internalized prohibitions against self-expression, solitude will be difficult to feel, even if you're a hundred miles from another human being.

Each time you begin a Write, you're crossing a threshold into a place of utter safety, where you are free not only of distraction but, ideally, of judgment, censorship, the expectation of performance. You want to become absorbed by your thoughts, whatever they are, unconcerned for the moment about anything else. Look at this absorption as prayer space, meditation space, art-making space, anything that helps you thirst for that solitude in which you can hear yourself think. This is your sanctuary.

We know how difficult it can be to create a sanctuary in your home even under the best of circumstances, but especially if you have children or share a small apartment with someone. The first step is to find space you can use privately. It can help a great deal to talk to the people you're living with, explain to them how important it is for you to have this one half hour without interruption. Most people will honor that need if they understand it. You can find private space in surprising places. When we first taught Proprioceptive Writing to groups of college students, we were amazed at how resourceful they were in ferreting out space for their practice. They set up their candles and tape decks in empty stairwells, in dormitory laundry rooms, in the bathrooms at night! We hope you won't have to go to these extremes, but here are some guidelines to cut down on distraction wherever you are.

Even if you live alone, try to work in a room with a door that closes. Remove the telephone from the room or unplug it—you want to be "off the hook," literally and figuratively, for the next half hour. Do not bring coffee or tea or even water into a Write with you; stopping to sip is a distraction. You will be working at a table or a desk, seated in a chair, so you can assume a study position—comfortable, but not too comfortable. Attentive. Inward is a gesture, not a place, and to make it you need to feel relaxed, but also braced, self-contained.

CREATING RITUAL

Part of the power of Proprioceptive Writing lies in the beauty and safety of ritual. To create your own ritual, you'll need either a tape deck or CD player in the room, and a recording of

Baroque music, preferably the slower movements—largos, adagios, and andantes—that you'll play for roughly twenty-two to twenty-five minutes. On the table place a candle, which you'll light just before the music begins and blow out at the end of the Write. In front of you should be a small stack, perhaps four to eight pages, of white unlined paper. The least expensive you can find is perfectly adequate. You may want to keep a stapler and a folder nearby for the finished Writes.

It is these outer aspects of the practice—freedom from interruption, the soft intensity of the burning candle, the beautiful rhythmic quality of the music, even the whiteness of the unlined paper before your eyes—that set this off as a time and place in which to establish intimacy with yourself, to gather up attention. You don't need a workshop to create this ritual. You can do it on your own where you live.

WHY BAROQUE MUSIC?

Even in antiquity, music was recognized as a bridge to altered states of consciousness. In their 1979 book *Super Learning*, Sheila Ostrander and Lynn Schroeder discuss the various roles music plays in our ability to learn. They report studies showing that Baroque music has a calming effect on the body, including lowering blood pressure; that its slower tempos, which have roughly the same number of beats per minute as the human heart, shifts the brain off its everyday beta rhythms to alpha rhythms, which are more conducive to creativity and learning. According to the authors, composers of Baroque also wrote music with the idea that it opened the doorway to the mystery of

God and the cosmos—not a bad preparation, in our view, for spiritual renewal.

When Linda first started writing proprioceptively, Baroque music—and in particular, Bach—was what she selected, and it felt right. When she asked a friend, a Vermont painter, why he painted to Bach, he told her it was because he liked to think his ideas were as good as Bach's! For the first two years after Toby started doing Writes, he tried different forms of music but kept coming back to Baroque. Occasionally a student may complain that the music gets in the way of his or her writing at first. If you feel that way, we suggest you push ahead anyway. No doubt by the third or fourth Write you'll forget all about it. That's probably when you'll also begin to derive its benefits.

WHY THE CANDLE?

Candles are often used as a focusing tool in meditation forms, as well as in religious devotions. In Proprioceptive Writing, lighting the candle at the beginning of a Write is a way of creating a sacred space for your practice.

Even a single candle will generate a luminous glow that can quiet your mind, focus your attention, and help you turn inward. As you write, you want to be like the flame and burn with intention. Light the candle when you begin a Write and blow it out when you finish—this establishes a clear opening and closing to the session. Some proprioceptive writers like the ritual so much that they report having pulled off to the side of the road while on a long drive and having a Write in their car . . . complete with candle and music!

Here's a revealing experiment: After practicing with the candle for a while, try doing a Write without one. We guarantee you'll miss it.

WHY TWENTY-FIVE MINUTES?

Back in the seventies, when we were first experimenting with the structure of a Write, we chose twenty-five minutes primarily for convenience. Most people still used audiotapes, and one side of an audiotape was twenty-two to twenty-five minutes of music. But coincidentally, in many forms of meditation, including Zen and Transcendental, the suggested length of a sitting practice, especially for beginning students, is also twenty minutes to a half hour. Experience in those traditions show that if the practice period is extended much beyond that time, attention slackens. Once the mind loses its focus, you may start to think of the practice, even if subconsciously, as time-consuming or tedious and may be inclined to do it less regularly, or burn out altogether.

The same is true of Proprioceptive Writing. Better to establish a regular practice—at least five times a week—of shorter sessions than to do longer sessions less frequently. It's always easier to find a half hour during a busy day than an hour. Think of how many times you've talked yourself out of going for a swim or a jog because the whole process (warming up, getting dressed, etc.) would take an hour or more.

On the other hand, there's no need to be overly rigid. When the music ends, don't stop in the middle of a word. Finish your thought, or the sentence you're writing, and wind down to what feels like a natural close. Once you've established a good regular practice, occasionally you may want to try a longer Write—say, forty minutes. But as a rule, we think you'll find that twenty-five minutes is sufficient.

WHY *UNLINED* PAPER?

Using plain, unlined white paper for your Write is a gesture of freedom. With it, you are departing from the schoolroom that straight lines suggest and becoming the author of a more complex, perhaps messier, but inherently richer script whose movement and direction is entirely your own.

Part of what you're doing in a Write is discovering what you really think and feel as distinct from what you feel it's permissible to think and feel. If your thinking is riddled with "shoulds" and "oughts," you need to know that. Those little words are like the gnarled roots of a mangrove swamp; they twist around each other, threatening to cut off our air. As we like to remind our students now and then, thinking proprioceptively can be a subversive activity—you can use it to break out of this gnarly prison. You may find inspiration on this matter, as we do, in the words of Virginia Woolf, who said in an essay called "Street Haunting": "What greater delight and wonder can there be than to leave the straight lines of personality and deviate into those footpaths that lead beneath brambles and thick tree trunks into the heart of the forest where live those wild beasts, our fellow men."

We also recommend using only one side of the page. This gives more flexibility in organizing your Writes, as we will discuss in Chapter 6.

Use the moments just before the Write to slow down and turn inward. As you start the music, light the candle, and settle into your seat, you might say to yourself: Now I am about to write. This time is for me. What's on my mind right now? Is there a story I've been waiting to tell, an event I've been thinking about that I want to look into? A feeling I need to vent? A memory I want to explore? A puzzle I want to unravel? These questions can help gather your attention.

Once you're seated, but before you begin to write, take a moment to relax. Close your eyes and cup your hands over them gently. Wait till a black velvety curtain or purple field appears on the insides of your eyelids, or take several long breaths, inhaling and exhaling slowly. Many people find these moments an exciting part of the ritual, full of mystery and potential. We never rush through them, but savor them. This is your passageway into the Write, a time to become conscious of your opportunity. Now begin to write, following these three rules.

The Three Rules

1. WRITE WHAT YOU HEAR

Imagine your thoughts as spoken words and write them exactly as if you could hear them, as they occur to you moment by moment. This may be a little tricky at first because much of the time we go about our business unaware of our thoughts—

though, like currents in the sea, they're always present. You may not think in words but you can always turn thought into words. Anyone can learn to do this. So become an ear, a receiver of voice, a scribe to your thoughts. Slooooow down and turn up your hearing.

If you're having trouble writing what you hear, or even understanding what we mean by that, reread the section called "Putting Voice Back into Writing" (page 13). Think of thought as anything you might or could say, and say it in writing. For example, let's suppose you're confused about what you're doing in the Write. Treat confusion as a thought and say in writing something like "I have no idea what I'm doing here." If the subject on your mind is one you're already sick of or it disgusts you, treat that feeling as a thought and say it in writing: "I'm so sick of it!" You may be worrying, lamenting, complaining, scheming, boasting, defending, or accusing yourself or someone else, or simply noticing something—you can give voice to it all. Anything you think, you can say—however imperfectly. You have nothing to lose, since nothing you write will be judged.

Don't try to actively direct your thoughts or push them around; give the boss in charge of banishing socially unacceptable thoughts the night off. While the Master's away, become a receiver—receive, receive, receive.

Don't be concerned with grammar, punctuation, consistency, logic, fairness, eloquence, or any of the usual things you worry about when writing for an audience. Forget about introducing, concluding, or organizing your thoughts. To begin, don't wait for a special or important thought, one that is "worthy" of being written. Just start where you are. As we say to our students, "make a middle"; in other words, begin with whatever thought happens to be passing through at the moment.

2. LISTEN TO WHAT YOU WRITE

The skill that's most actively engaged during a Write isn't the writing skill at all. It's the hearing skill. It's hearing yourself. To hear your own thoughts and to awaken your auditory imagination, you must develop within yourself your capacity to listen. Thought can always be voiced, but to hear it requires a certain kind of intense, focused listening, a quality of attention: curious, patient, even-tempered. We call it the "listening presence." It never judges, edits, censors. It hears every thought—profound or foolish, hardheaded or emotional—with the same undivided attention. During the Write, you will be one or more of your thinking voices. And you will be that listening presence to yourself. This active relationship between thinking and listening is one element that makes Proprioceptive Writing different from other forms of process writing.

How do you delve deeper, get clearer about the meaning each thought holds for you? Sometimes you need a strong tool to help you stay attuned to your thinking and ask questions of it. The listening presence has only one tool, but it needs only one: the Proprioceptive Question.

3. BE READY TO ASK THE PROPRIOCEPTIVE QUESTION

The Proprioceptive Question is simple: "What do I mean by _____?" Into the blank goes whatever word, phrase, or expression that catches your attention. This word or phrase will change as you go along, but the Proprioceptive Question itself is mantralike; it never changes. Always be ready to ask this question at any moment during the Write, of any word or phrase you have written. Always write out the question, and write what you hear in response to the question.

The PQ, as we call it, is an attention-focusing tool. It helps you to amplify your thought, express it more accurately, and reflect on it more meaningfully. Like a magnet, it attracts thought. It draws out concrete details buried within thought. One student, Martha, compared the PQ to the lamp on a coal miner's helmet:

> *Whenever Linda and Toby talk about using the question to shine a light on something we've written, I have the image of myself wearing a hard hat with a light attached, like the ones Carter and I wore when we visited the mine in Bisbee. But in my Write I'm descending into the darkness alone, there's no tour guide, not knowing what I'll find. I hear a sound coming from the corner—a scraping sound. What do I mean by* scraping? *Maybe something frightening, like a rat. I turn my head toward the sound to light up the corner. I don't have to do anything else— the light is part of the hat, part of the turning. The question itself is that motion.*

When you ask the PQ, you are inquiring into the psychological or emotional sense the word has for you. Certain words arouse memories, feelings, attitudes in your consciousness; they are "charged" for you by your experience. The sound of a lover's name, for instance, carries emotional weight. If you're afraid of flying, the words *takeoff* and *passenger* may be loaded for you. The PQ enables you to unpack and investigate them, leading you down a path toward story.

Sometimes the PQ can lead into story with amazing speed, despite daunting barriers. Such was the case for David, a childhood refugee from Nazi-occupied Poland, who wanted to write a memoir of his early life but faced a real obstacle: He barely remembered anything about it.

We were aware of David's presence in the first few sessions of the workshop. He sat on the outside of the circle, concentrating hard and listening intently to others, but he had a dark and worried air about him. Then one day, in the opening passage of one of his Writes, we heard what David was feeling: "What will they think?" he wrote. David understood that in Proprioceptive Writing he was to write whatever he was thinking and probe his thought with the PQ. But as an accomplished scientist and teacher, he considered it vain and beneath him to care about other people's opinions. He was ashamed even to own up to it, much less explore it. Realizing that this reaction to his own thought was self-censorship, he didn't know how to proceed.

Finally, after a few Writes, David realized the importance of his mundane concern and heard that the word *they* was loaded. "When I worry about what they think," he wrote, "what do I mean by *they*? Who are these others with such power?" The specificity of the PQ immediately opened David's mind to his traumatic past and returned his shocking memories to him.

There is a large cast of them.

It is the winter of 1942. The ground is frozen. My mother and I just arrived in Mielneze. We found a room in a boardinghouse. I am outside. I am surrounded by four boys all older than I am. We are standing in an inner courtyard of the old town. The boys are all urging me to pull out my penis and masturbate along with them. I know that what they really want to see is if my penis is circumcised. Then they will know I am a Jew. I run to tell my mother. She examines my penis, tries to pull the skin down. She manages to squeeze the skin together. She holds it down. Perhaps if she ties it down it will form itself into a permanent covering. This does not work. There is no way around this. My mother cautions me that I must keep my penis hidden. So this worry about "what they will think" is connected with fear of being found out. This is a repeating pattern.

We arrive in another town. A group of boys are playing on the street. They come up to me. Do you want to play blindman's bluff, they ask. I am really happy that they want to play with me. They blindfold me. They hand me a stick and tell me that I should start chasing them. I feel something wet and slimy on the stick and it stinks. I realize that the end of the stick I am holding is covered with shit. I am embarrassed by my trustfulness but also I am overwhelmed with rage. What do I mean by embarrassed? It's the feeling of being found out, that I am defenseless, that I can be had. What do I mean by rage? Rage for me comes in various grades from one to ten. A one is when people are chewing popcorn while I am trying to watch a movie. A ten is shoving a shit-covered stick in my hand.

Now other memories flood my mind—the German soldier; the man who pushed me off the train; the man who shot my father; the other side of the story—the cast of people who saved me.

By imagining himself as a boy in the midst of boys and the object of his desperate mother's tactics, David learns what he means by *they*. The concern with what people will think was no mere vanity for a Jewish boy trying to pass as a non-Jew in Poland, 1942. That younger David had to keep his head or risk disaster. "What will they think" was a life-and-death question. Amazingly, asking the Proprioceptive Question of the simple word *they* threw open the doors of memory, and stories began to flow.

How often should you ask the PQ? As many times as you want or need to. Ask it whenever you sense emotion or story in a word or phrase you have written, when you want to analyze your thought, or simply when you have a hunch something juicy is lying in wait for you. Over the years, hundreds of people have come to us because they wanted to go deeper than they had been able to go with other forms of process writing. Time and again they tell us that it's the Proprioceptive Question that makes the difference, that allows them to dig deeper and answer that desire.

At the end of twenty-five minutes or so, the music should stop. Finish writing out your last thought. Don't worry if you haven't tied everything up neatly or didn't say everything you wanted to say. You'll have many more Writes and many more opportunities to return to those thoughts if you wish.

THE FOUR CONCLUDING QUESTIONS

Before blowing out the candle, write down the following four questions and answer them in writing. Sometimes your answer will require just a few words, and sometimes you'll want a fuller response. This is often where revelations occur in the session. Take the time you need for this. These questions are an important part of the Proprioceptive Writing ritual, so don't hurry through them or cut short your answers. Remember the joke about the airplane pilot who contacted the control tower. "I'm lost," he reported, "but I'm making good time."

1. WHAT THOUGHTS WERE HEARD BUT NOT WRITTEN?

Cast your mind back over the last twenty-five minutes. Did a thought or a feeling come up during the Write that you didn't or couldn't get down initially? One that maybe you didn't feel comfortable with? Or dismissed as trivial or irrelevant? Or simply didn't notice? Remember, flashes of feeling or quick visual images are among the forms thought takes, and should be mentioned. This question is not asking what you *might* have written, but what in fact you thought and did *not* write. Ask this question in the same spirit as you might ask yourself, when writing down a dream in a dream journal, "Did I get all the parts of the dream?"

2. HOW OR WHAT DO I FEEL NOW?

Find the word or phrase that comes closest to your emotional state at this very moment. Do you feel drained, angry, stirred up, ashamed? Or calm, as if you'd just exhaled deeply? Are you more confused and muddled than before? Chances are you're not, but be honest with yourself. Don't always expect to feel better after a Write than you did before, especially at the beginning. You may have mixed emotions about what you've just written, or feel disturbed, or a little surprised at what just flowed from your pen. Think of it all as grist for the mill and write what you feel.

3. WHAT LARGER STORY IS THE WRITE PART OF?

Every thought is part of a larger thought. Every story is part of a larger story. This question asks you to imagine the larger container of *personal* meaning to which the thoughts you've just written belong. For instance, if part of your Write includes an argument about money you had with your husband the night before, what larger story might you be hitting on? Is it one of control between you and your husband? Is it the resentment you felt as a child because you never had "enough"? Is it a political story about power, a gender-related issue? Even if you're not sure, write down what your gut tells you.

4. WHAT IDEAS CAME UP FOR FUTURE WRITES?

In the course of asking and answering the previous questions, did any ideas or feelings come up that you might want to explore in a future Write? Put them down here. Though you should never hold yourself to a subject just because you decided in advance to think about it in your Write, you might find it helpful to begin a Write with one of these ideas. A student of ours once referred to this process as a "daisy chain of connection."

These final four questions complete the Write. Now blow out the candle, staple your papers together, date it at the top, and place it in a folder that you use only for this purpose. If you were writing in a workshop, you could now read your Write aloud to the group if you wanted, listening to the reading with the same focused attention you used as you wrote. Often, when you hear yourself speaking your thoughts aloud, emotions are aroused that were not called up when you were writing. Even if you're alone, we suggest you read your Write aloud so that you can hear your thoughts again in your own voice.

The Write Is Perfect, Even If the Feelings Are Not

Don't worry if you're not happy with your Writes when you first begin to practice Proprioceptive Writing. People sometimes view first attempts as meandering, uninteresting, or just plain badly written. Some are embarrassed or guilty about something they wrote. They may feel they have betrayed someone they love, or spoken too harshly. They may want to distance themselves from the feelings or attitudes the Write expresses, or disown them altogether. Such fear of expression is remarkably common; it stems from the unconscious assumption—really a superstition—that we alter circumstances by expressing or denying thoughts. In Proprioceptive Writing, the expression of thought is always valuable for its own sake. Like biofeedback, it transmits information from ourselves to ourselves. Expression is the route to discovery. Enid, for example, discovered that her daughter's unfeeling response to her was something she learned from Enid herself. After railing against Amanda for several Writes, on the fourth Write Enid got the message:

What do I mean by wrong? *It was wrong for Amanda not to call me when I broke my leg. How much have I ever asked of her? Now that I really need her attention, she's too busy to answer my phone calls, let alone run the simple errands I can't do for myself. Doesn't a mother have any rights at all? What do I mean by* rights? *Listen*

*to me carrying on. I sound so bitter. So hard-bitten. Boy,
is that voice familiar! It's my own voice. Oh, I'm quick to
get up on my high horse and complain about my daughter, but how do I respond whenever Amanda asks me to
baby-sit for her? I'm always too busy. I have a book to
write.*

Resist the temptation to revise your Write while reading
it through. The Write is perfect no matter how it comes out
and no matter how you feel about it. It's only a snapshot of
your thoughts at a particular moment and doesn't represent
your considered judgments on the subject. As we say to our students, you're not responsible for your thoughts. You don't
choose them, so don't feel guilty or sorry about them when you
report them. If at the end of a Write you find you touched upon
something that feels uncomfortable—or wonderful, for that
matter—you can say so in the four questions. You might in a
later Write find yourself exploring the same thought or feeling
from a different angle, one that brings up a different set of associations and observations.

SOME COMMON CONCERNS ABOUT
PROPRIOCEPTIVE WRITING

Even after you've learned the basic structure of Proprioceptive
Writing, you may feel for a little while that you're not "doing it

right." Try to relax. You can't learn anything new if you're tied up in knots about how you're performing. Try not to think of your practice as a performance at all, but as an organic process from which you will learn over time. Still, important questions do come up. Here are some that people often ask at the beginning.

Is the goal of a Write to get past self and write of other things?

No, you never "get past self" when you are writing proprioceptively. What you want to discover in Proprioceptive Writing is how you experience your life, what you've thought and felt in other times and places, and what you think and feel now. You want to stop reacting and start reflecting, stop hiding and start revealing. You want to use your own thought-flow and the feelings it carries in its stream to gain self-knowledge.

Why should I go through the ritual and write down my thoughts since I already know what I think?

The mind contains depths and mysteries that may not be readily known. How do you remain open and attentive, day after day, month after month, to the subtleties of your thoughts? Even if you're absolutely sure in advance what you'll produce in a Write, you may be surprised to find something else emerging. If you become an empathetic and curious listener overhearing a speaking voice, an unexpected aspect of yourself may surface. If you listen imaginatively and ask the PQ, you may discover unsuspected motives, conflicts, emotions, or attitudes.

Can I make an agenda for the Write before I begin?

Yes, you may make an agenda, but be willing to let go of it if your thoughts take you in a different direction. As we often tell workshop participants, "make sure it's a personal agenda"— that is, one that comes out of an emotional need to say what you're feeling or hear what you're thinking, rather than a subject for a composition.

What do I write about?

It's that little word *about* that makes this question tricky. Every piece of writing intended for an audience is about something. But a Write is a literal record of your reflections and reactions, written as they occur to you, moment by moment, during a particular half hour, not a deliberated essay. So write what you're thinking. Write what you're feeling. Write what interests or concerns you. Write your explorations into meanings. Examine your associations to your thoughts and write them. Whatever you think: write!

What if I don't like what I'm thinking? What if it bores or frightens me?

In Proprioceptive Writing, we define feelings as forms of thought. Like attitudes, beliefs, opinions, and judgments, feelings can be expressed as words. If you are reacting to your own thoughts with fear and boredom, express these feelings first. Then get active with the PQ. Keep in mind that you don't have to like your thoughts to benefit from writing them down. Make up your mind to simply accept whatever impressions, ideas, judgments, or fantasies come to you when you do Proprioceptive Writing, no matter what. Some days your thoughts may strike you as boring; other days they produce Writes that may bowl you over with their power. Don't keep score. What you'll learn through a longer Proprioceptive Writing practice is that every thought has its place.

Should I keep the pen going all the time?

It's not necessary to write nonstop. Don't push the pen; let the pen respond to you. Some people pause briefly if a number of thoughts are competing for their attention and they're not sure which one to pursue. When the music changes mood or tempo, some people pause briefly to find their direction. What's important is catching what you're thinking, whatever it may be—not producing a constant *gush* of writing.

Do I have to write out the Proprioceptive Question each time I use it?

Yes, write it out. This simple task helps you to s-l-o-w d-o-w-n. When you think something you do not write, you make a little hole in your mind that other thoughts can fall through. So treat every thought with equal importance and try to catch everything.

How many details do I write down after I've asked the PQ?

There's no right number. We often tell our students that they have to find a balance between going forward and going back—that is, between writing what they hear and asking the PQ. If details are coming, stay with them until you're next ready to ask the PQ of another word or phrase.

Can I write for more than twenty-five minutes?

Yes, but there's no need to do more. On the other hand, if momentum is moving you, allow it to carry your writing along for a few extra minutes. When it levels off, complete the Write with the four questions. Always bring the Write to that formal close.

Do you ever go back and edit a Write?

No, never. The Write is perfect as it is. Editing is a very important task in formal writing but it has no place in Proprioceptive Writing. Though you can sometimes lift from a Write an idea or string of sentences to develop into a piece of formal writing, the two kinds of writing are quite distinct, as we've said before.

What about reading my Writes to someone who hasn't written with me, or doesn't even know about Proprioceptive Writing?

To read a Write to another person is risky, in our opinion, especially to someone who isn't familiar with the process of Proprioceptive Writing. Mostly, their comments are not very useful to you and may even do you harm ("You sound depressed. Are you?"). One misguided response—even a seductively positive one such as "Wow, that's good writing!"—can undo the work you've just done. *Proprioceptive Writing isn't about good writing.*

If you must read from a Write to someone else, at least be clear to your listener why you are doing so—for example, to share a thought; not for advice or approval. One exception: It is sometimes helpful to bring Writes into psychotherapy sessions, as some of our students do, since Writes contain information that may be useful to your work there.

Can I use other kinds of music?

Try practicing with Baroque for the first three months, for the reasons we discussed earlier. Then, if you like, experiment. A number of people we know have used Indian ragas with good results. Avoid music with words since lyrics compete with your own thoughts.

Can I use a computer?

Only if you experience discomfort holding a pen or pencil in your hand for twenty-five minutes. The computer encourages speed, not the slowing down needed for reflection. What you need to do in Proprioceptive Writing is slow down, not dash ahead. Being a bit of a purist about the practice also helps to separate it from everyday, businesslike work.

CREATING A PRACTICE

Now you know how to have a Write. To begin a practice of your own, try to write at least five days a week for three months. Doing it less frequently makes it difficult to see changes in yourself.

You want Proprioceptive Writing to become a positive addiction, and regularity is part of the process.

Another way to reinforce your habit is to practice Proprioceptive Writing at roughly the same time each day. Many people find mornings best, when their minds are clearest and before they've gotten tangled up in other events and responsibilities. Others look forward to doing it after work. The important thing is to be intentional about it. Plan for it and protect your time vigilantly. You will soon find yourself hooked. Once this happens, the practice will nourish you and make you strong. You'll stop fighting the form. You'll stop wondering if you're doing it right. Your life will become a moving path. You will write because you need to, because your happiness and serenity depend upon it.

Chapter Three

Self-Expression:
The Method as a Path
to Better Writing

O, reader! Had you in your mind
Such stores as silent thought can bring,
O, gentle reader! You would find
A tale in everything.
—WILLIAM WORDSWORTH

A few years ago, a colleague from our Pratt days, a devoted teacher and fiction writer, invited us to a party in her new Manhattan apartment. The rooms hummed softly with the voices of writers, artists, teachers, and social activists. At one point in the evening, our hostess introduced us to a small group of writing teachers at schools in and around New York, and spoke knowingly of our work. A little later, one of those teachers buttonholed us in the kitchen. "I might send you a few of my students," she said, almost conspiratorially. "They're good craftsmen, but their work lacks . . ." she searched for the word, "newness? sincerity? depth?" She never did find the exact term for what she meant, but it didn't matter. We knew what she was talking about.

In fact, we were encouraged by this woman's response. Many writing teachers we've spoken to over the years believe that while certain technical skills, such as organization and editing, can be taught, the more internal qualities a writer needs— empathy, voice, imagination, vision—are beyond the reach of a writer's education. They think you're either born with them or you're not. But we've always believed that these qualities can be cultivated in a beginning writer and burnished in an experienced one; we've seen firsthand that Proprioceptive Writing can accomplish this.

Not everyone has the desire or opportunity to write. But everyone has something to say and the potential of saying it in writing. Indeed, as Montaigne, the great French essayist, said, "Every man has within him the entire human condition." But how can we express such knowledge, whether in writing or any other form of creative work? Fears of every sort flatten and strait-jacket writing: fear of personal exposure, of self-contradiction, of being wrongly judged, of triteness, of sentimentality. In reaction, many writers seek what seems easy solutions to their problems, like flashier characters or distracting plot twists, rather than drawing on their own inner resources to literary advantage. They settle for too little too quickly, in our view. Yet we have seen writers of all levels of experience extend their thinking and enrich their worldview through the regular use of Proprioceptive Writing; in short, they overcome the many limitations that fear imposes. In this chapter, we'll look at how a number of writers we've worked with have done just that. Let's start by discussing the principal differences between Proprioceptive Writing and formal writing, by which we mean writing intended for publication, and how one can act as a preparation or stepping-stone to the other.

The Pleasure of Pure Process

As many of you already know, formal writing is hard. Creating a work of memoir, journalism, fiction, or some hybrid form takes enormous effort, which seasoned writers recognize. The outline doesn't hold. The structure collapses. Your subject, which seemed so engaging and solid in your mind when you started out, seems trite and meaningless now that you're committing it to paper. Your language feels fake and shallow. Suddenly the task appears monumental. Who would want to read this? you find yourself asking. Will it ever be published, let alone make money? Is all this just a waste of time? With questions like these swirling in your head, your confidence starts to fail, like a folding chair collapsing under you.

Beginning writers sometimes imagine that sufficient talent or experience eliminates these hardships. It doesn't. Many of our workshop participants are professional novelists, poets, and playwrights, and though they may anticipate difficulties more than new writers, and thus not become as overwhelmed by them, they, too, wrestle with demons throughout their writing lives. Ironically, the added pressure of success and the increased expectation that accompanies it can sometimes generate a more crippling brand of anxiety. Lofty literary positions and countless awards offer little protection against these fears. The author Ralph Keyes opens his book *The Courage to Write* with the story of E. B. White, who even after he'd reached national fame for his graceful essays and children's stories, still fretted over every word. "He rewrote pieces twenty times or more, and sometimes pleaded with the postmaster of North Brooklyn, Maine, to return a just-mailed manuscript so he could punch up its ending or rewrite the lead."

Many writers report that by doing Proprioceptive Writing on a regular basis, they're able to enter their terrifying feelings about writing and bring them down to size. And they do this on the spot, at their desk, without losing a day or a week or a month of work. Whether they are experiencing anxiety or not, some writers begin each workday with a Write, then segue into the formal writing project at hand. They use Proprioceptive Writing in a nuts-and-bolts way, as a warm-up, a problem-solving tool, a technique for working through issues their text raises. They use it as a way of figuring out the answer to that unnerving question, "Just what am I writing about here?"

Part of the magic of Proprioceptive Writing is that even as it prepares a writer for the difficult task of formal work, it delivers creative pleasure. Because Proprioceptive Writing is not done for a reading audience, and so does not have to meet aesthetic standards, it frees the writer from the pressures of performance. Even though you don't harness thought for a literary end in Proprioceptive Writing, you still perform essential writerly tasks:

identifying raw material, making it available for creative use by gaining distance on it, becoming accustomed to thinking in narratives, discovering and establishing voice. The continual use of the Proprioceptive Question helps you summon memory, explore experience, and develop the habit of attention to language and detail. And yet you never *compose* a Write. Rather, it comes into being simply by following the ritual and rules of the practice.

In fact, one of the simplest ways Proprioceptive Writing prepares a path for the formal writer is by developing the discipline that's required to establish a regular writing ritual. If you ask any professional writer, "What's the most important thing you can do to ensure your success as a writer?," the answer is usually the same: Write a lot. If you sit down for a half hour every day, or nearly every day, over a period of months or years, to do Proprioceptive Writing, you are creating a space in your life for writing. And while many professional writers describe the work they do as "slow" and "agonizing," most people report that the ritual of Proprioceptive Writing feels good. It's energizing to feel words pour directly from your mind, unimpeded, without concern for style or effect on an audience. Formal writing requires that you constantly make choices and decisions with the reader in mind. In Proprioceptive Writing, there is none of that pressure; you can indulge your own thinking— always a pleasurable process. When the work of formal writing begins to feel like drudgery or torture, Proprioceptive Writing can release you from the rack of decision-making and remind you why you wanted to write in the first place.

GETTING PERSONAL WITH YOUR SUBJECT MATTER

A piece of writing rarely springs fully formed from a writer's mind, but is composed and goes through drafts. The raw material of formal writing may live within you for a long time in purely private ways (you may dream of it, talk about it, take notes on it in diaries and journals) before you recognize its potential to serve as a subject for writing. But working toward a first draft of a finished work, and then from draft to draft, means that you must limit your thoughts and make them conform to a shape and a logic. In formal writing you have to control your material, decide what it is you want to say, grasp a point of view and the voice to express it. Left unresolved, any one of these matters can delay a writing project for years. Proprioceptive Writing helps here, too.

One of our former students, a journalist and published nonfiction writer named Jessica, was blocked for years on a project she yearned to write. Her paper had assigned her to Saigon during the Vietnam War. The city had changed her and she wanted to write about it in a personal way. But as a trained journalist, Jessica always tried to keep her writing impersonal. She wrote of other things—the political situation, the devastation of villages—but never the Saigon story that was close to her heart.

Writers who can't delve into their own experiences are deprived of one of the most gratifying aspects of a writer's work: the sense that who you are is making its way into your art. The work is deprived as well. When you are unable to get personal with your subject matter, you rarely get your story right.

As it happened, on the third day of a Proprioceptive Writing workshop, and through the use of the Proprioceptive Question, Jessica backed into a first-person account of her experience in Saigon, the very approach that had felt taboo to her before. Within that Write the mature, successful Jessica bumped into the young Jessica as she was starting out in Saigon in the seventies—and found the story she wanted to write about herself.

Saigon was hot and crowded with refugees from the cool, quiet countryside. Thousands of rebuilt motorcycles spewed their putrid smoky stench into the already dense air. What do I mean by Saigon? *Saigon was a girl, not a city. Saigon was the big leagues and I was a rookie.*

After all those years, it seemed miraculous to Jessica to hit upon the voice and point of view she had been searching for. At last she had her strategy for writing a personal story. Although the piece that she developed from this experience has not yet been published, it served as a watershed for Jessica's writing career. She told us more than once that her many other published pieces shifted after that Write and became much more gratifying to her.

Like Jessica, many writers find in Proprioceptive Writing a method for unlearning old lessons. Journalists, technical writers, and academics especially are often boxed in by the ideals of pure objectivity in writing. But while all writers must gain distance from their material to make use of it creatively, at the same time they must be involved in it, engaged with it personally, or they will be unable to sound the depths of their subject. With practice, these writers discover how to locate their raw material in themselves and become intimately familiar with it; how to gain verbal precision; how to digress yet stay on target. Because it gives them a regular place and time in which to engage their personal experience, Proprioceptive Writing has proven invaluable to professional writers like these.

STREAM OF CONSCIOUSNESS?

When we describe Proprioceptive Writing to people for the first time, many think it sounds similar to the "stream of consciousness" writing they may have studied back in high school. Isn't that a kind of spontaneous writing, they ask, one that rolls out from the pen exactly as you are thinking it and brings forth your innermost thoughts? The answer is no, but to understand how Proprioceptive Writing is different, the goals of "stream of consciousness" writing are worth looking into again.

As long as we live and breathe, we all have an inner life of some sort. Everyone has ideas, perceives the world, suffers pleasure and pain in a way that makes one oneself and not someone else. The term *stream of consciousness* was first coined about one hundred years ago by William James in his seminal work, *The Principles of Psychology*. What it refers to is the ongoing here-and-now of thought—the ceaseless activity of perception that is happening now, and then now, and then now. "Let us call this the stream of thought, of consciousness, or of subjective life," said James.

As a literary technique, stream of consciousness was given its stature by the talented authors who employed various forms of it—Dorothy Richardson, Virginia Woolf, James Joyce, Gertrude Stein, Jack Kerouac, among others. And indeed, the prose these writers produce *seems* to emulate the way the mind works when uncontrolled by outside forces, where the "stream" is a series of ongoing thoughts loosely bound by their association of feeling, idea, sound, or image.

But let's not forget that artfulness is involved here. Stream-of-consciousness writing does not emerge spontaneously out of the unconscious or flow forth freely from the writer's pen, though he or she may succeed in convincing us otherwise. Rather, this flow is devised to sound like interior thought. The author is *simulating* the experience of consciousness deliberately and for a purpose: to tell a story, to render a worldview, to reveal a character's interior or subjective life.

To be a writer, and especially to write out of your own life, you must be imaginative about what it's like to be *you*. It is not enough to spill words, even intriguing or provocative words, onto the page. Writers have to penetrate experience. Many students, when they first work with us, fail to distinguish between their real inner world and mere verbal patter that sounds unscripted. This happens because they are writing how they think stream of consciousness should sound, based on literary models, rather than what they are really thinking. They cannot believe that their ordinary perceptions and sensations, those that speak of their own experience in the world, could be the stuff out of which literature is made. Proprioceptive Writing teaches them that this is exactly what it is.

WRITING OUT OF YOUR OWN LIFE AND IMAGINATION: THE TRIALS OF A BEGINNER

We met Nicole at a Proprioceptive Writing workshop we were running in Maine. Always a voracious reader, with a long-standing interest in writing, she had worked as an assistant editor in a publishing firm for several years after college, helping other writers improve their manuscripts. Then she married, had children, and put her career ambitions on a back burner, taking odd jobs to supplement the family income. Now she was in her forties, and with the kids in school and more time for herself, her desire to be a writer was regaining momentum. She even harbored a fantasy, rarely shared with anyone, that one day a book of hers would be published—perhaps a novel, or a series of autobiographical essays.

But Nicole was in a quandary. Earlier that year she had attended a memoir workshop at a highly regarded writer's conference, and the instructor had delivered some sobering news: personal experience alone, no matter how interesting or true, did not a memoir make. The week before, Nicole had attended another workshop at the same conference, but that teacher made no distinction between formal writing and the kind of personal, autobiographical writing her students were doing, and so was happily positioned to applaud all their heartfelt offerings. She never challenged them to control and shape their raw material with an outside reader in mind. When some of these students, including Nicole, took similar work to the tough-minded second teacher, she showed them that what they had created was, as she quaintly put it, "home movies"—narratives of interest to the writer and perhaps a small circle of family and friends, but not many people beyond that.

Nicole was left wondering: What elevates experience above the purely personal? What do "home movies" lack that the "big screen" requires? Which, if any, experience of her own would be worth writing about, and how would she gain perspective on it anyway? She really didn't know.

Nicole told us flatly that "nothing interesting" ever happened to her, and that was part of the problem. What she meant was that she hadn't had many life experiences that seemed to her dramatic or noteworthy. She hadn't traveled to any exotic locations, or seen angels, or gone through any near-death experiences. Hers was a relatively ordinary (she often used the word *boring*) childhood, free of serious dysfunction or complication— no divorces, no alcoholism, no sexual abuse. And working for years while raising her kids, constantly responding to the demands of others, Nicole felt she hadn't attended to her inner life.

In the months between the conference on memoir and the Proprioceptive Writing workshop, Nicole came up empty when she faced the blank page. Although she could be entertained by the fiction and memoirs she read, she was certain no experience of hers could entertain anyone else. She couldn't seem to create subject matter not based on her own experience. She thought she might have something interesting to say about her family relationships, but when she tried to give her feelings about them substance, they seemed elusive. How much did she want to reveal about herself, let alone the other important people in her life? And who'd be interested in these "home movies" anyway?

Only on rare occasions, in response to the pressure of powerful emotions, could Nicole write convincingly about the people around her. And when she did, it felt disloyal. After all, it involved complaining, laying blame, revealing secrets about her imperfect family—*in writing*—all of which seemed dangerous and even wrong. Yet in these moments she wrote with clarity, verve, and a confidence in her subject that was inaccessible to her at other times. This confused Nicole further: she wrote when she was driven to it, but in the clear calm of her desire to write, she was blocked.

Like many people who want to be writers, Nicole had a fraught and twisted relationship to writing. She worshiped writing. She feared writing. She longed to write but avoided writing. Nicole was a writer who didn't write. Writing was her nemesis and her joy. She appreciated the difficulties of craft: to say things rhythmically, expressively; to shape the story in a voice that feels true. But Nicole wasn't ready to approach these practical problems. She was facing a more vague, existential angst. Could she take herself seriously as a writer? Did she want to do the *work* of writing, or was she seduced, as so many others seemed to be, by the promise of entitlement the label "writer" carried? In spite of her age, could she become a beginner again?

We got to know Nicole a bit as a writer that summer. Her problem wasn't that she didn't have anything to say, or that she lacked the imagination to say it, though she tried to convince us it was. With so much anxiety built up around the act of writing, Nicole had become frozen, cut off from her own voice. To regain it, she needed first to open herself to her private thoughts, right or wrong, as they occurred to her moment by moment. She needed to trust her own perceptions and engage them, without worrying if they pleased or impressed anyone else—not judge them for their literary worth. Proprioceptive Writing was a good place for her to start.

Rushing Past Experience: Nicole's First Write

On the first afternoon of the workshop, Nicole produced a Write that she read to the group. She thought she wrote honestly, even confessionally, but still she wondered if it would interest anybody. She hadn't censored, as far as she could tell, but the Write seemed meaningless and dead-ended. She read softly and with embarrassment at first, but gained confidence as she went on:

Everyone else at the table seems to be writing so diligently— so involved in what they are saying. I wonder if I really belong in this group. I don't know what I'm supposed to be thinking about. Will I lose control? What do I mean by control? *Will things come up that I'm not willing to deal with? There's so much to say. Can I keep up with my thoughts? Is that part of the process—to train the mind to bring out some sort of structure? Thinking of the music now, and taking piano lessons as a kid. And my father watching me with a big grin on his face, then something happening, and him getting angry, then my getting angry at him. Jim is easy to get angry at. But do I want to go into that? I need to trust in this. I feel like I'm writing big, like a baby. What do I mean by* big? *Jim says I make a big deal out of everything and maybe I do but I feel I keep everything in. What do I mean by* big deal? *God, I feel like I've had about three cups of coffee. I'm afraid to stop, but am I doing this right? I have to let it come out. What do I mean by* it? *The anguish and hurt. Well, I'm doing it. But will I follow through? Will I ever really write anything? Or am I just doing therapy? The music is pulling me along; it's incessant; it won't pause or stop. I have to keep writing; if I stop I censor. What do I mean by* censor? *Like right now, I'm clenching my teeth, I'm putting up a social front. How much information should I give about myself? Why would it interest anybody anyway? It doesn't even interest me. And what about Jim and the kids? Is it fair to them, the writing I mean? I hope he finds the dinner I left for him in the fridge. Now I sound like my mother. This was his first weekend off in a long time and I feel guilty about leaving him. Is guilt what binds me to Jim?*

What thoughts were heard but not written? *None that I know of. Well, one: I thought, Am I hearing this or just saying it?*

How do I feel now? *Frustrated. Glad the music stopped.*

What larger story is the Write part of? *I don't know. A wife's story?*

What ideas came up for future Writes? *Don't know.*

Before Nicole can entertain the question of what use this Write can have to her as a writer, she needs to ask herself if she is engaging her experience or racing by it. In this Write, Nicole records a flurry of passing thoughts, perennial worries, confused feelings, but she's impatient with herself. She's writing about feelings but feels nothing about what she's writing. That's why, even at this early stage in her practice, she rightly wonders whether she has "heard" this Write or merely "said" it. To say what she knows in a voice that sounds real—the job of every writer—Nicole needs to slow down and interact with her thoughts. She needs to use the Proprioceptive Question not just perfunctorily but, in the spirit of a detective, with genuine curiosity.

Self-*expression* is more than just a gush of uncensored feelings. It's also an exercise in *reflection*. As we saw in Chapter 1, when you practice Proprioceptive Writing, you are constantly alternating reflective and expressive gestures. While you are completely free to write whatever you happen to be thinking, you are also asked in the Write to listen to yourself and be ready to reflect on what you are writing. By "reflect on" we do not mean judge or critique, we mean hold the thought in your imagination and scrutinize it. As you learned in Chapter 2, the tool that helps you illuminate your thoughts is the Proprioceptive Question, or PQ. The PQ brings information into your field of awareness. It also slows and focuses your thinking by making you look more closely into your statements and the language you're using to make them.

Even a Write such as this first one of Nicole's, on the surface so unpromising, is teeming with potential interest, which she could discover if she'd slow down and use the Proprioceptive Question. For example, Nicole asks early in the Write whether she'll lose control. Perhaps "things" will come up, she says, that she's not willing to deal with. What is Nicole referring to? She knows more than she's saying. In Proprioceptive Writing workshops, we often speak about "PQing" a word—that is, revealing the emotional content of a word or phrase by exploring it with the Proprioceptive Question. To find out more about the thoughts she's controlling, Nicole might PQ the word *things*.

A little later in the Write, Nicole wonders, Am I "doing this right"? Why wonder this? Perhaps Nicole feels as if she's back in school and taking a test in Proprioceptive Writing. If Nicole PQs the word *right*, she might discover a school story that she's never expressed narratively.

A scene from Nicole's childhood does enter her mind at one point during the Write. She flashed on a piano lesson she took as a child that caused anger between her and her father. This story is important; otherwise it would not have stayed in her mind all these years. Even if she has told it before, this is her chance to get it down in writing—in enough detail to mark it in boldface in her mind. To do this, Nicole might explore what she means by *anger* or *piano lesson*.

Nicole mentions her "anguish and hurt." In what experiences are her anguished, hurt feelings embedded? If Nicole responds to this question imaginatively, and PQs *anguish* and *hurt*, she just might unearth a good story. In the Write, Nicole raises the question, Does guilt bind her to her husband? Talk about a scary thought! Guilt has a thousand faces. What face does guilt wear in Nicole and Jim's marriage? She may feel torn between her loyalties as a wife and mother on the one hand, and the challenges confronting her as a writer on the other. Is Nicole's desire to write selfish, or is her failure to pursue her dream self-sacrificing? Like most of us, she cares about the opinion of others, perhaps too much. Is her conscience suppressing some of her desires? To bring these back to the surface so she can get a good look at them, Nicole might PQ *guilt*, exploring the word as she used it in the context of the Write.

When people first understand how immensely useful a tool the PQ is, they often tell us that they lie in bed wide awake at night asking the Proprioceptive Question of every word that goes through their minds, finding another story to tell for each.

This first Write felt stilted and inauthentic to Nicole, but not because she lacked an experience to write about. Rather, because she didn't *dig into* her experiences with the PQ. Her thoughts jump around helter skelter—from father, to husband, to the other workshop participants, to her prospects as a writer—looking for a place to drop down and engage, but they never do. Instead, they skim the surface, like brief items on the six o'clock news. Nicole felt she was expressing herself honestly, and she was. She just wasn't reflecting on what she was saying, and so rushed by her best material. If she slows down, she will find the kind of experience that carries meaning to her as a writer, experience that is concrete, evocative, revealing, and perhaps juicy.

FACING OUR THOUGHTS WITHOUT FEAR

At the heart of Nicole's problem is a common dysfunction we call *cognophobia*, a Latin term that translates literally as "fear of thinking," but by which we mean fear of facing our own thoughts. Since a writer must feel comfortable expressing herself in words, letting them flow from her before critiquing them or subjecting them to examination, many people who have an ambition to write are held back at the starting gate by some form of this condition. But why would we have this fear?

For one thing, we may mistakenly believe that by putting

things into words we make them happen, much as babies believe that covering their eyes for peek-a-boo makes them disappear. If I fantasize a loved one's death, I fear it may come to pass. In Nicole's case, what might happen if she writes about her anger toward her father or ambivalence toward her husband? She discovers that she doesn't love them? That she'll always feel this way about them? That she is a rotten wife or daughter because of her feelings? Some kinds of "magical thinking" are so ingrained in most of us, it's tough to break the habit. If you've ever knocked on wood or censored your words in order not to jinx your plans, you'll know what we mean.

Another reason we sometimes fear facing our thoughts is that we may assume doing so obligates us to act on them. For example, I may suppress my sexual fantasies about my friend's spouse in order to protect myself from acting on them. A surprising number of us would just as soon avoid starting down the slippery slope that uncomfortable feelings can present if we give them full expression on paper. Better to ignore or suppress them, lest they start to make our lives more complicated than we can handle.

Like Nicole, we often make the mistake of thinking there is safety in unconsciousness and danger in awareness. But the reverse is actually true. As writers, awareness of our thoughts gives us control over our material, whereas unconsciousness controls us. Thought transcribed as speech, expressed in writing, and explored proprioceptively loses its magical power over us. We discover that our words are only words, and not the last words we will speak or write on the subject, either.

Gradually, by practicing Proprioceptive Writing, Nicole learned to bring thoughts and feelings, even unwelcome, embarrassing ones, into words with guiltless regularity, much as one brushes one's teeth. By listening to and examining her thoughts without the burden of being responsible for them, or, worse, having to act on them, she became less self-conscious and less afraid to reveal details about herself and her family. The steadier her practice, the more imaginative she became about her experience, and the more expressive she felt as a result.

An Exploratory Mind-set

Another common way writers get stuck initially is by judging their ideas before they have time to develop. Before she has even let loose her thoughts, Nicole worries, "Will I ever really write anything? Or am I just doing therapy?"

In 1788, the German poet and philosopher Friedrich von Schiller wrote to a young writer who was complaining of feeling frozen and unproductive. Schiller's words have become famous in discussions about creativity and speak to one of the primary purposes of all process writing forms, whether free writing, journal writing, or Proprioceptive Writing: to prime the mind by freeing the voice from the silencing effects of premature judgments.

It seems a bad thing and detrimental to the mind if reason makes too close an examination of the ideas as they come pouring in—at the very gateway, as it were. Looked at in isolation, a thought may seem very trivial or very fantastic; but it may be made important by another thought that comes after, and, in conjunction with the other thoughts that may seem equally absurd, it may turn out to form a most effective link. Reason cannot form any opinion on all this unless it retains the thought long enough to look at it in connection with the others. On the other hand, where there is a creative mind, Reason—so it seems to me—relaxes its watch upon the gates and the ideas rush in pell-mell, and only then does it look them through and examine them in a mass. You critics, or whatever else you may call yourselves, are ashamed or frightened of the momentary and transient extravagances which are to be found in all truly creative minds. . . . You complain of your unfruitfulness because you reject too soon and discriminate too severely.

To open ourselves to our imaginations is the first step and sine qua non of creativity in writing—everything else depends on it. Though our minds are, by nature, open systems, they often close down by the time we reach adulthood, if not to information from the world around us then to information from the world within ourselves, a condition that deadens our sense of creativity. How do we get it back? How do we gain admission to those "momentary and transient extravagances" Schiller is talking about?

Unlike the process writing forms that admonish us to "Keep the pen moving!" and "Don't think, just write!" in the hopes of capturing thought on the run, Proprioceptive Writing is specifically designed to slow thought down and allow us time to explore it—and *not* judge it. Learning to assume this kind of exploratory mind-set, and practicing it each day, are aspects of the method that are helpful to writers, and at the same time pleasurable. Literary creation, or creation in any form, in its early stages particularly, demands an exactly similar attitude.

In practical terms, however, perhaps to get the project going and completed, we decide too quickly what to write. Personal exploration can be disturbing (assuming we know how to embark on that exploration) and, like Nicole, we're impatient to get on with it. So we settle for preconceived ideas that are already familiar to us. Of course, any subject we choose to write about must be limited in some ways—no piece of writing is about everything. But to impose limitations prematurely, before we've explored the wide and varied meanings our subject has for us, is deadly to the writer in the early stages of a work; hence, Schiller's friend's complaint.

In his response, Schiller wasn't telling his friend that he should give up writing, but rather that reason must relax its watch upon the mind's gates and let every thought pass through, to such end as may be decided later. In the exploratory period, as Schiller says, the writer has no basis on which to judge the usefulness of the thoughts and sentences he is producing. That comes later. For now, one could say that our principal tasks are to suspend judgment and maintain openness. Proprioceptive Writing improves our ability to do both.

DEVELOPING THE HABIT OF ATTENTION

Writing requires the habit of attention. Through the regular use of the Proprioceptive Question you define and redefine the words you use. You get particular, you get careful, you make more demands on your language to say what you really mean. If you prolong even the smallest of details before your awareness by engaging the PQ, it will open into other details and carry you *into* story. Compare, for example, Nicole's first Write with the Write that follows, which she wrote a few days later. As you'll see, utterances that may seem empty when you rush past them open into rich detail when explored proprioceptively.

I have my period and I feel crampy and raw. What do I mean by raw? *I mean that something is right there at the surface, almost within reach, not quite, not quite. And the music starts and it brings tears to my eyes. It is not a sad piece, but it pulls something out of me. What do I mean by* something? *I want to reach inside and pull it out, it is like an itch I can't reach to scratch, a tickle. What do I mean by* tickle? *My father used to tickle me, used to tickle all of us, and it was all in fun—to a point. But he didn't know when to stop. Or did he, and kept doing it anyway? What do I mean by* doing it? *The bottoms of my feet, he would tickle the bare bottoms of my sensitive feet, and then it would be enough, and I would beg him to stop, but he would only hold tighter, and cross my ankles in such a way that I would roll over on the bed, on his and my mother's big soft double bed, and with one giant hand hold my ankles and feet immobile while the other hand tickled and tickled. And my laughter would turn to screams for him to stop, and then to gasps for breath, and then I couldn't breathe, and I was begging him between gasps, to stop, please stop. And still he tickled. And he was laughing. And I wonder if he was a sadist. What do I mean by* sadist? *Someone who enjoys the pain of others. Did he like it? Why didn't he stop when I told him to?*

What do I mean by stop? *Sometimes we would be driving in the car, country roads, after a big dinner, big hills, bumps gone over fast so that you felt your stomach, and I, or my mother maybe would tell him to slow down, and he would laugh and speed up, another bump, and there goes my stomach and did he really want to see my dinner all over the backseat of the car? Did he get pleasure out of torturing us? "You must take piano lessons because I regret that I didn't." And when I refused he yelled at me, upstairs in his room, with the piano teacher waiting downstairs. The music just paused and I panicked, really, almost panicked, that this Write would be over, and I still have more to say. I must say this, must get this out—and good, now there is more music—and so the piano teacher is waiting right downstairs, and my father is yelling at me about the lessons. And he squeezes my cheeks together hard, so that the little wires that stick out the backs of my braces are digging into the soft insides of my cheeks, and he doesn't see, doesn't know, doesn't stop. And as if to make a point, he jabs his finger hard into my belly, as if pounding on a desk for emphasis, but this is no desk, this is my soft belly, this is that place by the diaphragm where breath comes and goes, and he is punching at it, right at that soft spot, with his stiff angry finger, and my breath goes, knocked right out of me, the wind is knocked right out of me, and I can't catch my breath, can't even tell him to stop.*

What thoughts were heard but not written? *Who was my father really? I loved him and yet in the Write I kept wondering who he was.*

How do I feel now? *I am crying and I want to make sounds, but I don't want to draw attention to myself, so I stuff the sounds and just let the tears run down my face.*

What larger story is the Write part of? *I don't know. Right now I'm just sorting out my feelings about my father. All I know is I haven't really begun to write about my anger at him yet. I haven't begun even to look at it.*

What ideas came up for future Writes? *Start looking at it.*

In her first Write, Nicole used the PQ mechanically and to
save herself from the calamity of going blank. Here she slows
down and uses it to unearth information that's buried in
memory. As she begins, she feels raw and crampy and senses
something on her skin. An itch? A tickle? The simple act of
writing down a thought necessarily brings attention to it. Then
she fixes upon a word or phrase and enters it (*raw* feels charged
for her), and that, in turn, opens up another scene, feeling,
memory, or question. Her recollection of her father's tickling
her and refusing to stop, for example, brings her to the memory
of his driving the family car over big bumps in the road and en-
joying their discomfort, which brings her to the memory of his
forcing her to take piano lessons, and then to the remarkable
detail of the little wires on her braces digging into her soft
cheeks as he squeezes them together.

As Nicole tumbles into the memory of her father's tickling
episodes, and associates the event with similar events, she has
what we call a Proprioceptive experience. She reexperiences
those moments with her father and is able to narrate how they
felt to her as they occurred. In doing so, she is able to imagine
herself as the child she once was and her father as a person separate from herself.

In a sense, what Proprioceptive Writing does is allow you to
hang out with your feeling and search for its source in situation
and emotion. Like Proust's *petite madeleine* and the flood of

memories that simple object evoked for him, in this process you, too, will become aware of details you thought you had long forgotten or never knew you had. You'll see colors of the walls, furnishings in the room, the shadows on the carpet where you stood. You'll hear sounds in the air, feel the sweat on your skin, a finger jabbing at your belly. You'll recall the thoughts that raced through your mind as that moment transpired. The "memory" becomes alive for you—a place you can get inside of and experience again. As one of our former students once described it, "The Writes have unlocked meanings, opened up memories I thought I'd lost, granted access to huge dusty rooms in old castles that are scary and fun to explore. For years I thought I had no memories, must have killed all my memory cells by injudicious living, or simply had told all my stories so often they were used up. Now I go inside those memories in Writes, and it's like getting the times themselves back minus the anguish—infinitely better than the movies."

Nicole was developing a sensitivity to her own language. If you think of language as a door to meaning, she was learning to open it. When she's ready to make writing decisions, she may find a way to use the tickling narrative. For now, reliving past experience in the forward movement of the present, and feeling the emotions of childhood with the resourcefulness of an adult, she is positioned to better see her family situation and to respond to it more thoughtfully.

Nicole is beginning to realize that the stuff of writing need not have exotic origins; the universe, in the shape of her own life, provides all she needs. Now she recognizes her father's actions as personal choices he made, not as blind forces operating on her. No longer under his control, she wonders: Who was he, what made him tick? This is no longer just a daughter's question, it is a writer's.

What Larger Story Is the Write Part Of?

One of the four questions we ask at the end of a Write is, "What larger story is the Write part of?" *Everything* you write is part of a story. *Every* story is part of a larger story. Events and experiences exist in relation to other events and experiences. Many writers work by constructing unified wholes out of separate pieces of experience. Imagine the content of your Write as a small part of a possible whole, a larger story you may not yet have conceived but which you may return to and develop later. Eventually, once you have come to understand what larger themes your stories illustrate, you will be able to construct out of your experience many "wholes" that have meaning for others. Let's take a look at a case where this question led to a finished formal work.

Rhoda, a designer of children's toys who wanted to write formally, had what she called "a pointless Write." She had wanted to work on an article for a professional journal but various distractions had kept her from it. In a fit of frustration, made worse by anger at herself, she had a Write, a small part of which appears here:

*And how to work at my writing anyway? Today every-
thing looks terrible to me. The house needs a paint job,
the furniture is too old to be comfortable, we need a new
heating system it seems, the vacuum cleaner is starting to
smell bad again. And everything I do, I do hating it.
Will I ever get down to the work of writing and when?
And now that the weather is nice, how will I keep myself
indoors? I just want to have fun. What do I mean by just
want? I want all work to be fun. It's unreasonable, un-
realistic. What do I mean by fun? Not frustrating. Fun
would mean being able to walk away from hating everything including wanting to kill myself over hating.*

Rhoda uses this Write largely to unburden herself. But some
clarity comes to her as she reflects on the final four questions. In
answer to "What thoughts were heard but not written?" she remembers a desire that had flitted in and out of her mind during
her Write: "I want to see Jackie so much. How will I ever get to
visit her?" Rhoda was missing a dear friend who had recently
moved to the suburbs. With everything on her plate—the over-
booked week of appointments coming up, the unanswered
phone calls—how could she possibly find time to visit her old
friend?

Rhoda's mind takes a surprising turn when answering
"What larger story is the Write part of?" "A time-disease story,"
she writes, already gaining a little distance on the material.

Eventually Rhoda wrote an essay called "Time Disease" that

was published in a women's magazine. We asked her to tell us how she made the leap from that question to the idea for the essay. "While I was busy venting in my Write," she told us, "other reflections were crystallizing behind the scenes. I was looking for clues to help me make sense of my frustrated condition because I've been in it so many times before. By focusing on minutiae, a greater knowledge of my situation was germinating underground. When I realized the real issue was missing Jackie, I recognized that my problem wasn't old furniture or smelly vacuums, but time. And that first quick hit of the big picture gave me the idea to write about time from the point of view of a person who always feels rushed."

Often, Proprioceptive Writers file their Writes in folders with labels based on their responses to "What larger story is the Write part of?" In Chapter 6, "Creating a Lifelong Practice," are suggestions for arranging Writes by theme to which you might want to refer later. These categories can be as generic or as specific as you wish—The Mother Story, The Work Story, The Marriage Story, The Uncle Harold Story, and so on.

Nicole, for example, placed many of her early Writes in what she labeled The Wife Story. As she wrote more and more about her childhood and adolescence, she created a file called The Daughter's Story. The names of files can also change. When Nicole's relationship to her own daughters became her focus, and she began to see her own life from a mother's point of view, she relabeled her "daughter" file The Mother Story. Now that file thickened, and included two generations of daughters and mothers, as did her file labeled The Father Story, which included Writes about her father, her husband as a father, and her husband as a son. Simple as these categories were, they broadened Nicole's sense of her subject matter, and helped her imagine her personal experience in larger human terms.

In fact, the more Nicole wrote, the more intrigued she became by the resemblances between her father and her husband and her mother and herself. Several months after that first Write, it dawned on her that what she wanted to write about had been in front of her eyes all along: the shaping force of one generation on the next. Through her Proprioceptive Writing practice, she not only discovered the raw material she wanted to engage with, but also how to step back from her subject to see what value it had.

As Proust once said, literature is a product of a different self, not a transcription of daily life. To write it, you must get creative about your own experience for the sake of the work. Once Nicole got distance on her feelings, she felt freer to serve the story, and less tied to her personal experience about it. And yet, if she hadn't had the opportunity to express the full range of her feelings through her practice, which you've seen a bit of here, she never could have appreciated the usefulness of her "home movies" and seen their potential to play to others on "the big screen."

Discovering Your Voice

David Ferry, a poet and translator, says about the poetry of Horace: "It's the voice that's the life of these poems: so free, so confident, so knowledgeable about himself and about work, so contemptuous of pretense, so entertaining, so joyful. The voice is an invention, of course, or a playing field of inventions, but it gives the illusion of speaking to us as we hear it with a startling familiar immediacy."

It's that "startling familiar immediacy" of voice that all writers seek to capture in their work. Voice, as Ferry suggests, means not the author but the author's inventions: the narrator or character who speaks in any work and whose speech is grounded in the idiom of class and time and place. Depending on the personality and attitude of a character, tone and diction will vary. They may be elevated, philosophical, comic, sophisticated, brooding, sardonic, wisecracking, ironic. But while diction and tone vary from story to story, essay to essay, or book to book, the necessity to project voice through writing is constant. It's voice that brings a work to life.

In writing a story or an essay or a novel, a writer may sometimes have to work on voice. But you never work on voice in Proprioceptive Writing. Voice emerges on its own when your feelings do not threaten you but are simply what they are. Authentic voice is born in that unguarded instant when you are imagining a situation you feel something about. You're not worrying about who your listeners are, or what they will think about you for expressing that feeling, or whether you must act upon what you have written.

In practicing Proprioceptive Writing over time, you will become comfortable with the play of your own voices, recognizing them *by feel* for how they sound (by their pedantry, generosity, self-pity, passion, peevishness, or whatever). Such recognition will be invaluable to you as a writer, and may well be the basis of your ability to create character.

Grant was a navy career officer and a marvelous teller of tales about life in the military. His whole being radiated personality. Everyone who heard Grant's stories encouraged him to write them down. Just speak into a tape recorder, they urged, then transcribe the tapes—you'll be published for sure! But once the words were written down, Grant's tone became flat, his diction was rhetorical. Gone was the unmistakable voice that had seduced his listeners and held them spellbound. None of the expressive gestures that helped Grant project voice in speech—imploring eyes, the use of his hands—could help him when it came to writing. He confessed that even his love letters to his wife had the ring of military reports: textbookish, jargon ridden, and stilted. Once pen was in hand, Grant the storyteller froze.

Grant came up to a weeklong workshop we were giving at our center in Rockport, Maine, one summer. Gradually, as he expressed his thoughts and feelings in his Writes, a moment finally came when he stopped writing the way he thought he was *supposed* to sound. He spoke in his own language, without concern for the impression he was making on the rest of us in the room. It was his seventh Write, and he'd been exploring his struggle to overcome "personal fears." When he asked himself what he meant by *fear*, this obsessed voice emerged:

What do I mean by fear? I seem to be frightened of damn near everything. If I'm not involved in conquering one fear, I'm engaged in a bout with another. I recall moments, still shots out of the past, when I rise above formidable odds. A fistfight with a west-side bully named Johnny Massina in which I received a terrible beating, but morally felt triumphant. I removed the bonnet nuts on a 650-point wet steam line once. There were only two nuts left containing all the energy that was driving a 10,000-ton ship through the Pacific. I sat astride the steam line laughing and the fellow working beside me turned yellow and split. He had won a Bronze Star in 'Nam as a forward air strike coordinator. I taunted him with a shout, "Where's your Bronze Star now, Buddy?"

You can't help but feel elated when a voice arises, as one of Grant's has here. Beforehand, you may have feared the aspect of personality that this voice reveals, but once a persona comes to life through your sentences, fear vanishes. As important as it is to read other writers carefully and observe how they create voice, nothing takes the place of hearing a voice of your own rise out of your written words. This is a high creative moment in any person's life and the true beginning of a writer's training in matters of voice.

Let's listen to another person discover a voice in writing. Miranda was an impassioned English teacher who often felt restrained by the elaborate bureaucracy in which she and her colleagues had to work. As a personal project, she wanted to write a firsthand account of the educational system as she was experiencing it. Yet while Miranda's teaching was natural and forceful, her writing was tepid, cautious, apologetic. The spirit of Miranda wasn't in it.

During one Proprioceptive Writing session, another student expressed anger at everyone who ever held her captive in the prison of a classroom. Miranda caught the bug. She felt rage, too! In her next Write, Miranda imagines burning down her old schoolhouse, and a voice emerges that she hadn't written in before:

So what do I mean by rage? *That schoolhouse stove was always tricky. Suppose I kicked it over (clad of course in an asbestos suit of righteous indignation) and the oil drum spilled and fueled a flashing explosion—the windows blew out while I watched gleefully from among the apple blossoms over by the ledge. The squeaking seats, the picture frame around Abe Lincoln, the wooden outhouse seats consumed. Generations of anguish cleansed by fire.*

The blackened granite steps, the slide and swing mere junk to haul away. No more Seabolt School. The townsfolk knew they had a monster school out there but let it be. Theirs be part of the guilt.

And now, what makes this cremation so important? I need to know that I am worthy. I need to be unbent to think aright of myself, to stand tall and move ahead for all of them to see. I am ready (am I?) to be strong and recognize the way.

Shout then a loud hosanna over blackened stones. Let old shame be burned out. Kindle your torch from the embers. For that which is finished is finished and what has begun has begun. Gloria in excelsis Deo and walk the child of shame down to the brook and sit on mossy stones to splash away the fearful chalkdust. Fold her in, put apple blossoms in her hair and sing a song:

Mine eyes have seen the glory of the burning of the school

We have burned the place entirely
We have broken teacher's rule
We have passed the righteous sentence
We have seen it melted down
It's time for marching on!!

By imagining herself as a vengeful student, the teacher in Miranda finds a crusader's voice. Miranda's willingness to be led by feeling calls forth this spirit. Ringing through the Write is the music of song and the purple prose of the preacher, sounds that had moved Miranda as a child, rising in her again.

Eventually, Nicole, too, developed a sense of voice through Proprioceptive Writing. She stopped watching herself, stopped trying to answer everyone at once. Notice how, in the following passage, the bored laconic tones of the speaker's voice convey the numbing repetitions of church ritual:

One of the benefits of this retreat so far is that I'm learning about community. What do I mean by community? *A community of writers. Is this going to be my Write about writing as sacred?*

What do I mean by sacred? *My head is bowed down in prayer. What do I mean by* prayer? *I am kneeling in church—in Christ Church—it is Holy Communion. Oh, Lamb of God, who takest away the sins of the world, have mercy upon us. The service goes on and on. We have to wait as each row goes to the altar. High heels clink. Shoes shuffle. My father pinches me when I wiggle. A hard, invincible pinch. It's easier to be still. The smell of perfume. A cough here and there. An eternity of waiting. Stained-glass windows. White tunic angels. Red Jesus on a yellow cross. A rainbow crown of thorns. Men in black robes move closer. The chalice of wine. The plate of wafers. A murmur, he died for us.*

On and on the service drones. But Mom has come to life. Having her sins forgiven has made her devout. She is kneeling. Her hands are folded. Her head is bent. The shiny polished silver offering tray comes by. We have our money ready. . . .

We stand. We sit. We kneel. We sing. Praise God from whom all blessings flow. We open the red book. We open the blue book. Up and down. Sunday after Sunday. Year after year. Men in black robes. Shuffling shoes. Clicking heels. Hard pinches for wiggling.

Believing that everyone speaks an entirely different language, the writer Frank O'Connor, as part of his writing training, tried to hear in his head the cadence of people's voices, the sorts of phrases they used in their daily speech. But not all the exercises in the world would have given Nicole or Grant or Miranda the confidence to write if they hadn't overheard their own voices and transcribed them. What's more, since it is impossible to separate voice and subject matter in formal writing, discovering their voices helped them find their subject matter. We have often heard writers say that once they find voice for a given work, the rest falls into place.

After months of Proprioceptive Writing practice, Nicole decided to write an autobiographical novel consisting of monologues, a form she'd grown comfortable with through her Writes. She based her characters on her parents, herself, her husband, and her children, but fictionalized them as well, incorporating into them elements of others whom she knew or imagined. In the end, she faced the challenge of making the family story believable, particularizing individual voices and sustaining them throughout.

This took more devotion than she thought she had in her. It took self-confidence as well. Occasionally the thought of an audience threatened to immobilize her. But the habit of writing that she had cultivated through her Proprioceptive Writing practice kept her working. Now, as before, she had to face the blank page and concentrate. But because of her increased powers of attention and her new self-knowledge, she managed to control her anxiety.

Nicole had reached the point where she was ready to grapple with the real challenges of formal writing and felt enlivened by the opportunity. Having been strengthened by the many days and months she had "met" herself in Proprioceptive Writing, she stopped expecting answers to be pat or desires to be satisfied quickly. She became more comfortable with ambiguity and more patient with herself. When she felt thwarted or unable to think, she recognized the source of her confusion. She resolved to outlast it: if her energy was erratic one day, it settled down the next. If her thoughts and feelings frightened her, she learned to coexist with fear. In time, her language became more precise. She gained control over her sentences. Her ideas took shape. Having thought deeply about her subject, she determined to complete a formal work of writing. Once Nicole had become an author in her own mind, she was able to begin her novel.

As the late writer and critic Alfred Kazin once said, "Language . . . is always failing and stumbling, breaking the writer's heart with its mere approximateness to the thing in his mind." Every writer wrestles with the difficulty of saying what he feels or thinks or knows. Students often complain that they are "inarticulate," but we don't accept this explanation. The question anyone embarking on the journey of becoming a writer must answer is: How much wrestling are you up for? As your practice of Proprioceptive Writing becomes more regular, you gain stamina. You learn that you're a worthy opponent who can pull to the surface of the page what feels buried or obscure. And you can do it with friendliness toward yourself and the world, and with the dedication that makes a writer.

Chapter Four

Proprioceptive Information: The Method as a Path to Emotional Health

---

Information is our source of energy; we are driven by it.
—*LEWIS THOMAS*, LIVES OF A CELL

For years we kept a Gary Larson cartoon taped to the wall of our office at the Proprioceptive Writing Center in Portland, Maine. It showed half a dozen aardvarks seated comfortably in the animal self-help section of the library, intently reading the following titles: *How to Avoid Natural Selection, Do It by Instinct, Dare to Be Nocturnal, Predator-Prey Relationships, Become One of the Herd.* Larson's irony, as always, was delicious. These aardvarks had mastered the school-taught tasks of life, like reading, writing, and library decorum. But when it came to their own instinctive aardvark behavior they apparently suffered a serious information deficit.

We humans, too, must sometimes turn to information from

outside ourselves to teach us what we should have the sense to know on our own. We have the capacity to know unaided who we are and what we feel. But somewhere on the way from childhood to adulthood we lose the knack of knowing ourselves inwardly, of learning from our emotions, of responding to the world in new and novel ways.

The symptoms of this disconnect are familiar: lack of self-trust, emotional and intellectual rigidity, fear of change, perfectionism, narcissism, addictions, and free-floating anxiety. In short, what the psychotherapy community throws under the wide umbrella of neurosis. This dis-ease is commonplace in our society, regardless of age or sex, race or class, education or income. The world we live in is its breeding ground.

When the pain of these symptoms reaches a great enough intensity, most people search for relief. Some search alone, some in groups. Some with the help of a priest or psychotherapist or guru. People call it variously a search for identity, faith, a spiritual path, self-expression, voice. However we name this breakdown in intrapersonal communication, repairing it is invaluable to us. Disconnected from ourselves, we cannot feel our true vitality.

In the Oliver Sacks story we looked at in Chapter 1, *physical* proprioceptive failure threw his patient Christina into a crisis. Information locating the position, tone, and movement of her body's parts—that is, proprioceptive information—failed to be transmitted to her brain and central nervous system. As a result, she lost her sense of body identity. She was not knowable to herself physically.

Not only our bodies but our minds can suffer from information deficit. Then the proprioceptive crisis is *emotional*: information about the feeling component of our thoughts does not reach us. In this state, we seem unknowable to ourselves. With a Proprioceptive Writing practice, you can forge a new path of communication to transmit information between your intellect and your heart. As an empathetic listener who is also the thinker and speaker, you can explore your thinking at your own pace and question the assumptions that have become fixed in your mind over the years. You can imagine new responses without having to act on them. You can allow yourself to express emotion without causing damage to others or feeling guilty. And because you can do all these things on your own while writing, you develop confidence in your native intelligence and trust in the way your mind works. In short, you can correct the information deficit that exists within you; you can become your own emotional healer.

PROPRIOCEPTIVE INFORMATION: GAINING THROUGH WRITING

To describe the kind of information we unearth in Proprioceptive Writing, we sometimes use the analogy of an archaeological dig. As in a dig, it's not just the found objects but information about a lost world that is conveyed by these objects that makes the dig truly worthwhile. Using the Proprioceptive Question—which many people, in fact, compare to a shovel—you can dig deep down and uncover lost or repressed emotion. The emotions brought to light through Proprioceptive Writing carry information that can change your understanding of yourself and the world.

Unlike ordinary nonproprioceptive information, which may simply add to knowledge without consequences, and unlike Oliver Sacks's use of the term to describe physical feedback that is conveyed automatically, in our sense of the term, proprioceptive information is something that comes through writing. It affects your understanding and feelings in a personal way. It broadens your point of view. It reveals the continuity between who you are now and who you once were, between the world that shapes you and the world you shape.

In fact, for centuries, anecdotal reports have linked writing, especially regular, self-exploratory writing, to emotional health. Since the 1980s, scientists have been testing these anecdotal claims and finding them valid.

In an article entitled "Writing About Emotional Experience Is a Therapeutic Process," for instance, psychologist James Pennebaker of the University of Texas reported the results of several clinically controlled research projects showing a relationship between disclosure of emotional experience in writing and mental and physical well-being. Interestingly, Pennebaker determined in his studies that if you write about feelings and emotions *without linking them to events,* or if you write about traumatic events *without linking them to emotions,* your writing is liable to make you feel worse. Pennebaker further demonstrated that writing that connects emotion to the details of an event, reflects on its significance, and assimilates its personal meaning induces a relaxed physiological and psychological state that has the effect of lowering blood pressure and improving immune system functioning. In 1999, a study by Joshua Smyth in the *Journal of the American Medical Association* reported that such writing could even alleviate symptoms of asthma and rheumatoid arthritis, conditions that worsen under prolonged stress.

We recall three students of ours, participants in a drug rehabilitation program, who used Proprioceptive Writing in conjunction with their therapy. When we asked them how it contributed to their recovery, one said ruefully, "It's harder to lie to yourself in writing."

We saw a good illustration recently of how people get health-giving proprioceptive information through writing. A woman named Louise had been coming to see us regularly in our private practice. She'd been working for years as a speech therapist in the public school system, but with school budgets being slashed and talk of layoffs in the air, she'd decided to become a speech coach for actors in New York.

The day before one of our sessions, Louise had lunch in a coffee shop with Willard, an agent who'd advertised himself as having "terrific Broadway and Hollywood connections." Louise harbored fantasies that Willard would introduce her to prominent theater people who might lead her to clients, so she agreed to pay his hefty consultation fee to get his advice. But it seemed to her that Willard spent most of their two-hour lunch dropping names and bragging about his own career in show business, which Louise didn't find terribly impressive. The practical strategies he offered seemed no more effective, she felt, than what she'd already picked up from several panel discussions at the local Y. By the time lunch ended, Louise was seething with anger. Yet she never expressed an iota of dissatisfaction to Willard. On the contrary, she grabbed the check, thanked Willard profusely for his time, and even left a large tip on her way out.

The next day Louise came to our session sick with self-disgust. She couldn't decide which she hated herself for more: concealing her anger from Willard or loathing him for dashing her hopes. "I never let people know what I really think," she groaned, "and then I end up furious with myself!" At that point, we suggested she imagine the previous day's situation through a Write. We asked her to be sure to use the PQ to bring out the thoughts that had gone through her mind as she and Willard talked.

I walk into the restaurant, full of excitement, and see Willard sitting alone, peering over his glass. He's gray and overweight and I feel let down. What do I mean by let down? *He can't do anything for me. I begin to feel hard. What do I mean by* hard? *He won't give me what I came for and I want to run out of the place, but I join him at the table and smile instead. I'm still hoping to get what I can from him. Then he starts to talk. I feel my impatience but I don't say anything. What do I mean by* impatience? *Like, I'm tapping on the table, making the tea in my cup spill a tiny bit each time my finger lands. He doesn't notice, he hasn't stopped talking for about twenty minutes. He hasn't even asked me yet what experience I've had, what my goals are. What do I mean by goals? Isn't it my future we're here to discuss, what I want to do with my career? He seems to be scrolling in his mind for something that will impress me, but aren't I here to impress him? God, I feel trapped. I begin to eat. What do I mean by* eat? *First the soup and the taste disappoints me. Then the bread and I'm angry because I'm eating without being hungry. I noticed he sucked his stomach way in when he went to the men's room. I'll show him, I think, when I can't stand the anxiety anymore, and then I take over. What do I mean by* take over? *I begin dropping names myself, my famous teachers, my schools and degrees, and I feel like I'm destroying him with my power. Then I see how pathetic he is. What do I mean by* pathetic? *He looked so desperate, so weak, I realized there wasn't a thing he could give me.*

Louise had a telling reaction to this Write. When she got to the second of four questions, "How do I feel now?" she wrote, "Calmer. Less dangerous to myself." In answer to the third question, "What larger story is the Write part of?" Louise said: "The story of two leaking boats. Now I'm feeling sort of sad for this man and even admire the way he keeps going. After all, his boat is leakier than mine!"

What information did Louise gain from this Write that softened her feelings toward Willard? When she relived the scene in the coffee shop, she experienced again her anger at

Willard, but this time she recognized her own pettiness as well. She realized she'd been unfair to him. For the first time, through her Write, she could see the situation she was caught in: using Willard to salvage her career, as he had been using her. Before writing she believed that Willard had trapped her into paying the check; while writing she discovered it was her expectations, not Willard, that had trapped her. Once she was able to admit to her own nastiness, she was able to accept her lunch partner's shortcomings. As we expected, the easier she was on herself, the easier she was on him.

When you're living through an experience, it's hard to imagine yourself outside it. But when you revisit it in a Write, you see yourself in a fuller context, which gives you information you didn't have before. You comprehend more about why you acted the way you did, why others acted as they did; in short, why what happened happened. You can recount the experience from a larger, more inclusive point of view, one which empathetically embraces the viewpoint of others, as Louise did as a consequence of her Write.

Perhaps you recall a situation from your own recent past in which you felt certain someone you trusted had wounded you, betrayed you, or taken advantage of you. It might have been a relative, a friend, a teacher or counselor. If such an event has become fixed in your mind, it's likely to come up in a Write. When it does, if you feel moved, take advantage of the situation. Reenter the story, telling it as you remember it, using Proprioceptive Questions to flesh out details and probe assumptions. Bring into focus the thoughts that went through your mind at the time as well as the meaning the incident has gathered since it occurred. If you examine your words closely, information may emerge that completely alters your sense of the story.

Learning to Become Present to Yourself

As we mentioned earlier, many of our students in psychotherapy examine their Writes with their therapists. These students report that Proprioceptive Writing intensifies the therapeutic process with which it shares many goals.

In the traditional therapeutic situation, the patient explores his or her thoughts and feelings in the presence of a listener who is patient, nonjudgmental, and empathetic. It is the therapist who directs that exploration, nudging the patient toward self-revelation. In addition, the ritual of appearing at the same place, at the same hour each week or each day, and speaking in the presence of this same listener, creates a safe place, which is vital for the kind of unguarded self-exploration that leads to change.

Proprioceptive Writing gains access, through its own ritual, to the same unconscious material that therapists work with. It creates the distance between the thought and the person thinking that therapists call *transitional space*—the space that allows for self-observation and discovery. Because Proprioceptive Writing captures thoughts and feelings on the page, it can help focus therapy sessions as well.

When I (Linda) was in my early twenties, I broke off an engagement with a young man whom I'd known for many years and assumed I'd marry. At that unhappy stage in my life I didn't know what I wanted. I couldn't even choose a short-term career path, and I sank into a state of depressed anxiety. I was lucky enough at the time to find a therapist who embodied all of the qualities we just described. I remember him as a tall, lean, empathetic man who did his best to make me feel at ease. In those days of strict Freudian analysis, where the "patient" free-associated and the "doctor" remained silent, my therapist was sort of a maverick. He believed thinking was work that changed consciousness. So we put our heads together and thought. With his encouragement, I found my life a bottomless source of anecdote. I never seemed to tire of peering into the pit of myself from the perch of an easy chair and reporting back the emptiness I felt inside.

Yet for all this, I changed very little. While in his company, feelings that were ordinarily oppressive to me lost their heaviness and became subjects of interest. As this happened, I became interesting to myself; revelation upon revelation broke in on me. But by the time I was a block away from his office, my old thoughts and feelings resurfaced. Sure, I was producing insights in our sessions, but so what? He was a skilled therapist, I told myself, and it was only his tact, careful questioning, and discreet observations that brought those insights to the surface. I could not claim them as my own, nor reproduce them, it seemed to me, except in his presence. If I was not performing for him, I felt my old sense of defeat return.

Fifteen years later, after I'd begun to practice Propriocep-tive Writing steadily, it finally dawned on me what had been missing from those therapy sessions. It was that very transi-tional space that therapists theorize about but cannot always produce: the space in which I could examine my thoughts seri-ously, noncritically, and on my own. In order to make the kind of changes I sought, I had to become open, nonjudgmental, and present *to myself.* And not just once a week or twice a month, but every day.

Wordsworth spoke of poetry as "the spontaneous overflow of powerful feelings" that originate from "emotion recollected in tranquillity." He was talking about the capacity of the poet to enter a state of mind in which he experiences himself simultane-ously as he once was and as he is now, a state in which he *feels* his emotions but is not overcome by them.

Proprioceptive Writing allows you the opportunity to enter that state of mind. When you experience conflict, as Louise did in the coffee shop, and cannot express it, you feel at odds with yourself, proprioceptively out of whack. But later, in the tran-quillity a Write offers, you can find words to express those emo-tions: your subjective experience becomes accessible to you. Like Louise, you can re-create the complexity of the experience, minus the conflict you felt on the spot. Away from the heat of the moment, you have the experience again, but this time with-out conflict or moral judgment.

This power to be at once yourself as you are now and in imagination as you once were is a capacity that every Proprioceptive Writing session helps you develop. It's what we call *becoming present to yourself*, producing the raw material of your thoughts and feelings while simultaneously listening in on yourself empathetically, inquisitively, and imaginatively. When you are present to yourself in this way, your attention is never divided; you experience no conflict or anxiety since you are merely recording your thoughts as they occur to you moment by moment. Then new information has a chance to enter your thinking. Because you're not blocking them out or defending against them, you can let go of old assumptions and ways of seeing that are holding you back. This process is key to your emotional health. We'll look more closely at how it happens in the next section.

BREAKING HABITS OF MIND

Thirty-five-year-old Ed is perpetually angry, most often at women, and his anger bursts forth at unlikely moments, like during discussions of where to eat or what movie to see when he's out on a date. He can't understand why he feels lonely and frustrated most of the time.

As if she had been wronged in vague or undefinable ways, Mary, an insurance executive and mother of three, seems dominated by feelings of resentment. She cannot seem to stop herself from taking it out on those closest to her through constant low-grade criticism. She doesn't know *what* she resents, and she often berates herself later for her actions.

Peter has a Ph.D. in molecular biology, but he's afraid to taste new foods, meet new people, or even try different routes to his office. Though he yearns to be more adventurous, everything seems to frighten him. He doesn't remember when he was free of fear.

What Ed, Mary, and Peter have in common is that they are stuck, locked into emotional responses that are counterproductive. Nothing intrinsic to their situations accounts for these responses; they arise automatically, out of habit. Something in Ed's preconception of women leads to his anger. Mary's misreading of the people close to her prompts her to mistreat them. Peter's presumption of ubiquitous danger reinforces his fears. Recognizing that their reactions are self-defeating is a step in the right direction, but this information is not enough to help them change. All three of them can offer rationalizations of their behavior. Yet when these fail to alter their situations, they become despondent.

All of us have habits of mind like these. A large part of what we call our "experience" is organized by these worn-out reactions. Because they have become so much a part of the way we see things, they seem impossible to root out. We may hardly be aware of them, but we are never completely free of them. To break old habits of thought and emotion, we need new information, a new point of view, a new story to tell.

If in a Write you see a trace of a habit, you might try to press that harder by asking yourself if there are particular people or situations that always make you feel, say, shy or angry or stingy. Do you feel a glimmer of recognition that you've been trapped with these feelings before? You may wonder why you've become entrenched in these responses, perhaps even recalling the first time you reacted this way. Do you remember how old you were, what time it was, whom you were talking with? Perhaps the way the room looked or how the air smelled will come rushing back to you.

Habits die hard, but it is possible to reroute old pathways of feeling into new thought. The ritual of Proprioceptive Writing allows you to examine the contents of your habitual thinking patterns, express the emotions they trigger, and like a camera drawing back to take more into its viewfinder, get the information you need to see a newer, broader picture. In the next few pages we'll look at how this process led two people to breakthroughs in understanding themselves.

Shaking a Feeling of Poverty: Jack

A tall, boyish man of thirty, with brilliant black hair and brown skin, Jack often feels downhearted and weary. He dreams of returning to school to study photography. He has been saying this for five years, ever since he started working in the electrical appliance firm his father began when he was around the same age.

But where will Jack ever get the time or money to pursue his dream? Intellectually, he feels inadequate because he "cannot build his mind." Professionally, he feels stuck because he knows he's not following his heart's desire. When will this condition ever change? He doesn't believe it will. Jack projects his history forward, generalizing it into a permanent situation. He feels no amount of time or money will ever be enough to get him what he wants.

It isn't until he has a lucky break—the chance to return to school, all expenses paid—that Jack realizes his emotional despondency is neither economic- nor time-based, at least not at its roots. Though he now has exactly what he says he's been lacking all these years, the feelings of deprivation and emptiness linger. In the Write below, he tries to figure out why:

Poverty. What do I mean by poverty*? Not enough. It's somewhere around spirit. Poverty of spirit. I'm wondering about this feeling of not ever having enough. It was last night at dinner, listening and speaking with Lara, Jean, and Carol, that I realized I was making assumptions about Lara. About her being able to go to school to study and to be taking this time to build her intellect, her mind. I was responding almost negatively, even though it's what I've wanted to do for so long! I have never felt I could do this. That I would always be having to work at the same time, to be split. What do I mean by* split*? To make money, to be split in pieces, not able to focus on just studying and taking myself seriously. At Mom's* *house last weekend I was talking to Beth about getting the money to go to school and get an MFA and was there a way to do it so that I didn't have to be working also. And then Mom called the next day to tell me she could pay my tuition out of my share of inheritance money from Dad, so that I didn't have to work—talk about getting what I want. And yet this old image of me is hard to rid myself of. What do I mean by* image? *The feeling I have of not having, of not being able to do what I want to do. To just follow the urges I have to photograph the life I see around me. It's so slippery, hard to get my hands around it. What do I mean by* slippery? *I see Mom standing at the entrance to the Art Museum. This is years ago. I have just introduced her to Isaac Valosh, the painting professor I am assisting for the day in Chicago with a group of students. I introduced my mother's husband, Ben. I said this is Ben, he's an architect. What is it I am trying to get at here? My mother's stance in relation to these men. How I introduced her. I said this is my mother, Susan Williams. I didn't say, this is my mother, she is a painter. I only thought of this later and felt sad about it. I'm not sure what it has to do with this feeling of poverty, but it does. This place of inadequacy and the way I feel . . . unavailable to my own intellect.*

What thoughts were heard but not written? *Something else about Mom. The way she stands, the way I see her standing in relationship to the men around her, even*

Dad, her talents dismissed. I see her looking up, not on equal ground. I want her to be on equal ground. I am disappointed that she is not.

How do I feel now? *A sadness in my chest, remembering this. On the edge of crying.*

What larger story is the Write part of? *Not sure exactly, something about her place in the world, my place in the world. Bits and pieces trying to find a foothold.*

What ideas came up for future Writes? *More on this poverty, this barrenness, this feeling that I can't have. I'll never have enough money to do what I want. What I want with my intellect.*

"Poverty" is the first piece of the puzzle that Jack lays down, the thought he hears that could hold a clue to the condition he is trying to understand. He monitors the word proprioceptively, and in this way catches by the tail some feeling about his mother, which leads him to the visual image of her standing at the museum. As with many of our students, Jack has an awareness of an image at an emotional level first. He *feels* this scene before he *sees* it. He brings it into focus by monitoring the language of feeling, in this case by probing the word *slippery*.

Jack's sadness, connected in his mind previously to economic entrapment, finds a new emotional pathway to his experience of his mother. What meaning is there in his mother's stance that day that makes Jack want to cry? There is shame in his sadness. Should he have introduced her as a painter, put her at the level of these other men, and why didn't he? Jack doesn't yet know all the ways his felt poverty of spirit are intertwined with perceptions of his mother's second-class citizenship. But he's beginning to sense a connection.

Jack returns to the scene at the museum in the first question, and this time expresses the desire he could not earlier: "I want her to be on equal ground. I am disappointed that she is not." Perhaps his mother's status in the male world of artists places her son's sense of entitlement at risk. Can he allow himself privileges his mother lacked, or does he feel destined to live out her deprivations? How mother and son are entwined in each other's lives at these deep regions Jack will discern more fully as he moves along. But the complexity of this scene and its impact on his emotions are becoming part of his reflections.

Prior to this Write, Jack lived this sense of lack as sadness, as a heaviness in his chest. "Poverty," "barrenness," "the feeling I have of not having"—these terms indicate habits of belief that Jack experienced as unchanging aspects of his nature. To bear them was his plight. Now the *thinker* in Jack is awakening. He knows that his time-and-money explanation for why he is stuck will no longer suffice. He has new information to work with that was unavailable to him before. Old assumptions still have a hold on him ("I'll never have enough money to do it"), but the power of that habitual thought is weakening.

Regaining a Lost Voice: Maria

Maria is a scientist in her mid-forties who speaks three languages fluently besides her native Spanish. Yet in the presence of people she perceives as "figures of authority," Maria reacts with the quivering heart of a little girl: She freezes in terror, loses touch with her ideas, and feels unable to speak. Like a proprioceptive blackout, this internal breakdown between her powers of thought and her powers of speech throws her into a crisis of identity. Who is she at these moments? Imagine her fright at such loss of self-control. Maria's highly competent public persona allows her to conceal her fear of collapse from others, but she cannot hide it from herself. At the time Maria took a Proprioceptive Writing workshop, she was living in dread of these episodes.

Like Jack, who explained his situation as a lack—of time, money, and spirit—Maria also misconstrues her condition as a form of deprivation. She believes that words are missing from her life. "Words, it is always my need for words that is on my mind," says Maria. "Always" is a telling term, revealing Maria's absorption with her symptom and the extent to which she feels subjugated by it. But words themselves are not the problem for this articulate woman. It is her sense of her situation, her assumption that she will be speechless, that's become entrenched in her mind. She needs to break out of this habit. As she discovers through this Write, an emotional complex that controls the flow of words is at the heart of her affliction.

I'm not sure how to begin this Write. I think I want to talk about questions of authority and power. Authority has always frightened me. What do I mean by frightened? *I feel small, without a say, just accepting whatever is pushed onto me. Without an ability to say a word, to express my feelings or my position in a given situation. I have this feeling often when I feel attacked. What do I mean by* attacked? *I mean not being understood, being interpreted differently from what I'm really saying, being given a label or being "spun" in a way others want to spin me, for their own purposes. It makes me feel so helpless, like I've lost any clear sense of myself, I'm just one potato at the bottom of a sack of potatoes. When I feel like this I want to say, no, that is not what I said, that's only your assumption, what I said is such and such. But the words do not come to my mind, to my mouth. And I feel helpless and angry. It is only later on, when I am re-living the experience, as I do over and over again, that I realize the thoughts are there because the words have come back to me, the words that will make my position clear, establish my identity. But it's too late!*

Words, it is always my need for words that is on my mind. Sometimes I find it difficult to speak, to let a flood of ideas come through the way they want. I always marvel at how easy that seems for some people, almost without conscious thinking. In some instances I can do that, too, and when the words do appear, I marvel at them.

> *Other times, in front of anyone who even unconsciously reminds me of someone with authority, I freeze. What do I mean by* freeze? *It's like something in me slows down and I cannot move. Even my tongue slows down and a fog seems to enter my brain—I can't think clearly. Sometimes my fingers tingle a little and my palms become clammy. When did this process start?*

"Authority" and "power" are loaded terms for Maria, but until this Write she wasn't even close to knowing what they meant to her. As she monitors the word *freeze*, she begins to identify specific bodily sensations: She slows down, her tongue gets heavy, her thinking fogs over, her fingers tingle, her palms become clammy. With this new information, Maria gains understanding she lacked before. She had wrongly believed that words ceased to flow because she didn't have enough of them. Now she's realizing that emotion throws an entire internal system into crisis. When she's unable to speak, it's because she's gripped by fear of authority. "Where did this process begin?" asks Maria.

Over the next several Writes, Maria explored images that began to flood her mind. At home, a kind but traditional father encouraged her silence, even as he taught her four brothers to speak up and defend themselves. In school, nuns frightened her with tales of fire and damnation. In response to these fears and to the figures who represented them, Maria "adapted," she says, and became a "good girl." What exactly she meant by good girl, and at what cost to herself, Maria started to explore in her fifth Write:

It's pouring out, the whole sky is smoky black as if it's late afternoon. It's solemn in here, like Good Friday. What do I mean by Good Friday? *We used to go to church at school, three o'clock mass. Lining up in size order, pure silence, the girls had to wear something on our heads, little black veils or our school caps. Those who forgot had to pin tissues to their heads. Remembering the first time, the only time I was punished in school. It was in first grade, Sr. Francesca's class. But it wasn't Good Friday, it was First Friday, we had to go every month. We were lining up to go into the church. The girl behind me asked me a question. I didn't want to answer her; we weren't supposed to talk. But she kept bothering me, kept asking me something. I whispered something to her and told her to stop, someone would see us. A minute later, Sr. Francesca tapped me and the girl behind me, and one or two others. She made us stand in the back of the church, facing the wall while everyone else filed in. I started to explain my innocence, but she just yanked me against the wall. What do I mean by* my innocence? *It wasn't my fault, I couldn't believe the injustice! I wanted to explain what happened. I started to cry, and the girl who got me into trouble called me a crybaby. I cried more, I couldn't stop myself, it was so unfair. I am tasting the salty taste of my tears now. My face burning with humiliation. We had to stand for the whole mass, and then wait while the whole school filed out again. Then finally she let us go. I was last, so she made me go through the church and pick up the tissues that had fallen off the girls' heads during Communion.*

What thoughts were heard but not written? *I thought Sr. Francesca loved me—how angry and disappointed I felt when she judged me so wrongly. If I could only explain, I thought. But I couldn't. I stood there and cried.*

How do I feel now? *A little shocked at how deeply I still feel this. Sad for myself, sad that it meant so much to me to have her approval, to be thought of as "good." Suffering so much for such a small thing.*

What larger story is the Write part of? *The life decision I made to swallow my feelings and keep my hurt to myself.*

What ideas came up for future Writes? *Need to look at other instances of this silencing. How do I recover my powers of expression?*

Recalling this girlhood scene, Maria uncovered a moment in her past when, forbidden to speak in self-defense, she lost her voice in a flood of tears. Recollecting that moment in the safety of the Write, she experiences the feelings she'd had then, the proprioceptive information that will be so useful to her—the strain of standing for hours in the back of the church, her sense of indignation at being punished unfairly, even the salty taste of her tears and the hot flush of humiliation. Though the years have given Maria some perspective on their importance ("Suffering so much for such a small thing"), the incident clearly still holds great intensity for her and is a clue to how she deals with those in her adulthood whom she considers authority figures: She freezes, hangs up the phone on herself, clamps down her own thinking mind, swallows her feelings. Though the strategy may have been adaptive in childhood, when Maria was under the thumb of powerful grown-ups, it has long since become habitual and is hurting her today.

Habits of misperception aren't easy to break. Revisiting one incident in a single Write won't erase Maria's discomfort with authority figures, just as Jack's recognition of his mother's compromised position as an artist won't restore his self-confidence immediately. But these Writes are beginnings. As Jack penetrates his "feeling of poverty," and connects it to his sadness over his mother's subordination to men, that heaviness in his chest begins to lift. As Maria realizes that her "problem with words" is shaped by incidents in her past, and that she can delve into those incidents over time, her hopelessness gives way to confidence that she can conquer her fear. For both of these individuals, these are crucial adjustments in self-perception and important first steps in getting "unstuck."

TRUSTING YOURSELF

A fundamental marker of emotional well-being is the capacity to trust our own minds. Yet often it seems distrust is our more common condition. The renowned pediatrician and psychoanalyst D. W. Winnicott, who believed that lifelong crises of self-confidence begin in childhood trauma, explains our distrust of our own minds as the result of the intellect being called upon to solve problems for which life experience hasn't yet prepared us. To regain a sense of control, children continually seek to understand stressful or traumatic events in their lives. Lacking adequate knowledge of the world to do so, they're left to create scenarios that seem plausible but serve no healing function.

In more than twenty-five years of teaching Proprioceptive Writing, we have come across hundreds of people who were punished or humiliated in school simply for their individual styles of learning and came to distrust themselves at their core. The more anxious they felt about learning, the more they continued to perform poorly in their own eyes, and the more inadequate they felt.

Perhaps the simplest, most overlooked explanation for the distrust we feel of our minds is the ongoing process by which we are severed from our intuitions about the world. From the time we are born, we begin making sense of ourselves and our world by building a body of experience-based knowledge. These experiences, and our explanations of them, are validated or modified first by our parents, then by teachers and other adult figures.

When as children our thinking isn't validated, we may start to lose faith in our own perceptions and thought processes.

It isn't always easy to validate the intuitions of those we are close to, especially if it puts us in a weak or imperfect light. Our friend Charlie, who by day is a buyer for Macy's, remembers that when his only son, Damien, was eight and at the peak of his burying-birds-in-the-backyard stage, he brought home an injured dove and tried to nurse it back to health in their basement. As it happened, Charlie had a terror of becoming trapped in closed spaces with birds. When he needed a lug wrench over the weekend from his tool chest in the basement, he called down to his son to bring it up to him. "Why don't you come down and get it yourself?" Damien asked, knowingly. Charlie thought for a minute. The picture of competence on every other playing field, he hated to be thought of as chicken by his son. "Because I'm afraid," Charlie finally answered, figuring it was better to put his cards on the table than to purposely mislead his son. "I thought so," said Damien. By making such a choice, even on a scale this tiny, Charlie was helping his child construct an understanding of the world from his perceptions—in this case, who his father was, including his irrational fears. Had he tried to fake his son out and lie about why he was avoiding the basement, Damien's intuitive reading of the scene might have been made problematic, a subtle undermining of his innate trust in his own thinking.

One of the most common signs that we distrust ourselves is that we value the perceptions of others over our own experience.

We're reminded of one student, who, in a Write, told the story of how she witnessed a theft on a train. She saw a well-groomed man, dressed in a business suit, lift a wallet from a woman's jacket, which she had left on a seat when she went to the rest room. When our student reported the incident to her college-age sons that evening, they dismissed her story outright, saying she must have been too far away to have seen the theft accurately. Besides, they argued, a professional man wouldn't risk getting caught stealing so overtly when he could more safely commit a white-collar crime. In the Write, she explored how doubts about what she saw started surfacing in her own mind, though she knew perfectly well that the man had stolen the wallet—she'd seen it with her own eyes! Her story was about how this knowing got eroded, and it led her to wonder about other life situations in which she gave in to the interpretations of others, even when they contradicted the evidence of her own experience.

Roger presents a moving example of someone who suffered from a lack of self-trust all his life. He was in his mid-sixties when he began practicing Proprioceptive Writing. The son of Japanese immigrants, he'd grown up on a farm in California, had served for several years in the army, and afterward had held a number of jobs in the corporate world. When we met him for the first time at an introductory workshop with his wife, Phyllis, he had just retired from a middle-management position in the aeronautics industry.

A warm and openhearted man, Roger was a little surprised to find that he needed the first two or three sessions to get comfortable with the Proprioceptive Writing format, which involved reading Writes in his wife's presence. After all, they'd been married for thirty-two years! Underlying those early Writes was the nagging sense that, although he was gifted intellectually and his career had been a productive one, something was missing. His life still felt "unlived," as he put it. In his fourth Write of the weekend, Roger stumbled upon an event from his childhood that he experienced as an epiphany. It illuminated an undeniable but indistinct feeling of failure and shame that had plagued him most of his life.

The Write began inauspiciously enough with some comments on the weather and how much he enjoyed listening to the Writes of the other participants. He especially admired the work of a woman whom he felt showed great courage in the way she engaged painful material around the death of her child. He said he didn't think he could ever survive such a disaster, and then, as he monitored the word *disaster*, this little story rolled out as if it had happened yesterday, much the way Maria's Good Friday story had.

> *I guess I was about five or six, probably doing some chore or another on the farm near the pigs' area, when I saw Bootsy, my cocker spaniel puppy, going into the fenced-in area where the pigs lived. I think at the time I loved Bootsy as much as I did my folks and my grandparents, who lived with us. Anyway, my brother came around and we started wrestling and the next thing I knew Bootsy was gone. I realized right then that the pigs had*

eaten him. I mean I knew about pigs, how mean and tough they can be, I was a farm kid. I leaned over the fence and called and called but no Bootsy, and so I ran, almost fell into the house, and told everyone that the pigs had eaten him. "Oh, no," my mother said. "Bootsy just went into the woods and he'll be back soon." Then I went to my grandparents and they said the same thing. Of course, Bootsy never did come back. Even then, I didn't really believe them, but their words stopped my crying [and here Roger began to sob] but I could never again trust anyone completely. I tried, I wanted to believe them in spite of what I knew. And now I don't even trust myself, have never really believed in myself since then, not really.

As moving as it is, Roger's story might be interpreted by some people as a typical childhood memory of a sad event. But for Roger it is much more than that. When he got to the third question, "What larger story is the Write part of?," Roger answered, with tears in his eyes, "The story of why I can never take that extra step to succeed." Over the next three Writes, Roger cataloged moments when his lack of self-trust cut into leadership possibilities, the way a certain tentativeness sapped his enthusiasm for what he was doing and put a wedge in his relationships with his colleagues and superiors. His examples were mainly from his professional life, but a couple stretched back to his time in the army and even in college. Roger's work in these Writes made it clear to all of us that if we don't consider our interior selves of primary importance, we don't trust the intuitions that come from them. If we are limited by self-doubt, we severely minimize the possibilities for joy and satisfaction in life. His work was by no means done, but he had come upon real, usable information, which made a difference in the way he perceived himself—the first step toward change. On the last day of our workshop Roger was glowing with pleasure, and his wife spontaneously announced to the group that, in spite of all their years together, she never knew her husband as intimately as she did now.

If you are one of those people who trusts the opinions of others more than your own, or if you consistently second-guess your most immediate reactions, you may want to see how it feels to assert your opinions in a Write. Does it frighten you? Does it make you belligerent? Perhaps you remember a time when a parent or a teacher whom you trusted humiliated you. You may find yourself recalling one of these instances and be drawn back into the experience of it. You may find surprising associations with the event connected to behaviors that cause you discomfort even today.

Sorting Yourself Out from Your Parents

As children we absorb our parents' psyches through our skin, including their fears and limitations. Often our identification with our parents continues into our adult lives and yields confusion and trouble. It's not surprising, then, that the material in our Writes frequently revolves around unresolved issues with the people who raised us.

Our parents are our first teachers and our interactions with them are more profoundly formative than our interactions with anyone else. How we feel about them matters to us our whole lives, affecting our relationships with others whom we love, in particular our own children. Even if we can praise our parents in general for the people they are and the job they did with us, it is a rare person indeed who harbors no anger or resentment toward a mother or father, or disappointment in them, or shame about them. If these disturbing emotions about our parents remain locked inside our hearts, we suffer. They conflict with how we wish to feel. If we never view our parents as complex people with lives of their own, we cannot really grow up. Proprioceptive Writing allows us to go back to these crucial relationships and reexamine them.

Deirdre was a personable, supersmart woman whose work life as an FBI investigator was a fiasco. Though she could outwit criminals and lawyers and was terrific at building a case, she found it nearly impossible to satisfy her superiors and was sometimes reprimanded for losing her temper. She was repeatedly passed over for the promotions she felt she deserved.

Dierdre's father, too, had had a reputation for smarts. He'd been a math whiz in high school who had wowed his teachers with his ability to do difficult calculations in his head. Yet he graduated from college without organizational skills or record-keeping discipline, and so was frequently fired from sales jobs when Deirdre was a child. He eventually started his own haberdashery business, but his company went under when he couldn't keep cash reserves ahead of expenses.

Dierdre now looks back at her father's inability to provide for their family with shame and embarrassment. At the same time, to her frustration and amazement, she realizes she's been following in her father's footsteps. She, too, is often erratic, impatient, and irresponsible at work. She has no idea why she has come to model her behavior on a parent who caused her so much pain when she was younger. In one of a series of Writes in which she tries to bring him into focus, Deirdre remembers her father through the eyes of that girl:

> *I'm angry at him now, but was I always? What do I mean by* always? *Before I wrote him off, when I was younger than I ever remember being. What do I mean by* remember? *When I think of him then, it's his energy that was so appealing. Even my friends in junior high used to comment on it. "Your dad is so sexy," they'd say, and at the time I'd be embarrassed by it, or maybe I was just pretending to be embarrassed. What do I mean by* pretending? *I thought he was sexy, too, but I didn't want to admit it, he was my father after all, and he was sort of a screwup. But he looked so much younger than his age and he had this carefree way about him, like nothing could worry him. When we'd go out to dinner, which was rare because we really couldn't afford it, he'd drive Mom nuts by leaving the waiter a ridiculously large tip. She'd roll her eyes and shake her head, but he'd always insist, it*

made him feel more powerful, I guess. I didn't see the in-securities then, or how Mom was getting worn down. I just saw his confidence. He was fun to be with. What do I mean by fun? *When I'd bring my math homework home, we were supposed to do it a certain way, it was called the long math. He'd show me the easier way, the shortcut to get the same result, and I'd say, we have to show all the work, do it the long way, and he'd laugh and say, "Why take the slow boat to China, if you can get there by jet?" So I did it his way and sure enough the teacher would take points off, but I didn't mind, I felt I had pleased him. What do I mean by* pleased? *Maybe I'm still trying to please him, show him I'm cut from the same cloth, the way I don't want to do the detail stuff at work, all that inputting of data to get the program up. I know it's important; Sandy has spoken to me twice about it and both times I sounded off at her. As if I'm afraid that if I do something the company way, the way I'm sup-posed to, I'm going to turn into the world's most boring person. Dad's not even alive for God's sake, but I wonder, am I still trying to impress him, to be his little girl?*

Deirdre is moving beyond her familiar feelings of shame toward her father and getting the information she needs to make sense of herself now. In this Write, she feels again what her life in those days felt like; she remembers the girl who once loved her father and why. In that context, against that backdrop, her emulation of him starts to make sense. In her boring suburban adolescence, he was a figure of rebellion and adventurousness, and so held great allure. The more she understands her early feelings toward him, the more slack she cuts him for his failures and the less shame she feels about their past.

This generosity enables Deirdre to cut herself loose from the patterns she inherited from her father. As a result, she's controlling her temper at work and becoming more aware of the forces that drive her. In "What thoughts were heard but not written?," Deirdre writes, "I can't keep pretending that I don't care when I'm passed over. I do. Who knows, maybe he, too, cared more than he showed. And even if he didn't, that's him, not me."

Over the years, we have listened to hundreds of Writes in which people complain of having been labeled as children lazy, stupid, dishonest, flaky, or fat. Sometimes, even thirty or forty years later, they are still trying to undo the damage. To shed the label, some have headed to the other extreme of behavior—the "lazy" person becoming a workaholic, the "flake" becoming conventional—to prove just how wrong their parents were about them. Proprioceptive Writing is an effective way to gain distance from these judgments and see what's underneath them.

Sometimes it's our judgments about our parents, not theirs about us, that we need to take another look at. Often we're not even aware of the way our lives have settled in around those judgments. They're like the background noise to our lives—we're not conscious of being perturbed by them, but we're not free of them either. In the Write below, Tim's perception of his working-class father, whom he's always held responsible for his own career failures, is slowly being reconfigured, and a forgotten love of him rediscovered.

Let's talk about climbing the ladder of success. What about this climbing business? Is there something about height that's too awesome for me? What do I mean by height? *Uncomfortable with, unworthy of, the loftiness. Nah, I don't believe that. It's something else. What do I mean by* something else? *Dare I say rising above my father's expectations? Well, let's see, what do I mean by* expectations? *Why did he always find fault? Always bragging about me to the rest of the world, the aunts and uncles, the guys at the shop. Even Father Reilly. But never a good word to me, ever. Why was that?*

Did he have ability? If he did, he chose not to use it. What do I mean by chose? *I mean he didn't because (1) he was lazy, (2) he was scared, (3) he was lazy. Okay, maybe lazy isn't fair. He put in long hours at the garage. But his mind was lazy. His goals weren't there. I remember his motto: "Don't knock yourself out." I loved him, I really did. He was a terrible role model. What do I mean by* terrible role model? *He couldn't make a decision to save his life. He lacked ambition. He opted for ease instead of challenge. I love him so. He took us to the ball games to see the Red Sox. Fenway was a few blocks away. Don't knock yourself out. . . . Baseball was a love we*

shared—that and quiz shows, "Jeopardy," "It's Aca-
demic." Gee, I never thought about it before, but was this
his latent intellectual side?

I think if he could have made a decision it would be
not to die when he did. But actually even that was pretty
great in retrospect. How many people have died while
watching their favorite TV show and weren't disturbed
in their death for two days? That's right, he got to close
up shop, settle in to his favorite easy chair, and do what
he does best, kick off his shoes and stretch out his feet! If
you had a chance to die that way, or go through another
year or more with the prospect of uncertain death oppor-
tunities, I bet most people would go like Dad did!

Am I being morbid? Why do I think this is so very
funny? I get this sense of him sometime, like he's hanging
around, telling me not to knock myself out. Maybe he
was real smart. Maybe he knew in the end it didn't really
make that much difference. Why struggle to give it all up
at the grave when you could give it up much earlier? Live
a life of ease, dedicated only to little problems easily dealt
with. What do I mean by little problems easily dealt
with? *I like the rhythm of the phrase. Like the customer*
who gave Dad a hard time about the brake job he did.
No problem. Dad could deal with that.

Even though Tim speaks here of his grievances against his
father—his laziness, his anti-intellectualism, his stubbornness—
and holds him responsible in some way for his own lack of

ambition, he sees that these resentments are old and useless. Tim is at a crossroads in his life. He is thinking about coming out and needs to put his own sense of failure behind him. Perhaps to gain courage for the challenges he'll face, he reconnects to an earlier period when his father was more than adequate as a role model—he was Tim's hero. In this Write, Tim regains the sense of the world that the boy and man shared. By the end of it, he has connected to his father's spirit on a deep level, and gives a full, rich assessment of his feelings: I love him so. After he speaks of the poetic rightness of his father's death, he feels a new harmony with the wisdom of his father's life. Maybe he was smarter than I thought, writes Tim with newfound wisdom of his own.

In the loosely affiliated community of proprioceptive writers, certain Writes are remembered for the emotion they arouse among the participants. About a third of the way into reading his Write out loud, Tim started to laugh. He couldn't stop laughing the rest of the way through. Perhaps because he was laughing so hard, we all caught the bug and by the end of the Write all fifty of us were in stitches. It was a release for all of us, not just Tim, and a reminder of the immense relief we can feel when we experience love for our parents in spite of our difficult histories with them.

It is now commonly accepted that emotions bear crucially on our health and overall well-being. Yet despite their conviction that this is true, many people are afraid of emotion and unsure of its value. Years of hearing proprioceptive Writes have demonstrated this to us. People worry that while some emotions are good (love, for example, or joy), others may be bad (hate or anger or jealousy). That's why we often tell our students: There are no bad emotions, only bad consequences from acting on them.

There is a difference between acting on and expressing emotions. When, in the course of writing or reading a Write in a Proprioceptive Writing workshop, an emotion rises—producing laughter or tears, turning skin clammy or hot, a face ashen or red—we discourage any attempt by our students to curb its expression or camouflage its significance out of fear or embarrassment. We urge them instead to allow their emotions full expression. Sometimes students worry that if they start crying, they'll never stop; if they probe their anger, they'll only exacerbate it. But emotions may have to intensify before they subside. It may seem a paradox, but it is nevertheless true, that every emotion is healthy—as long as it is felt in the presence of a calm thinking mind.

Chapter Five

Awakening to Yourself: The Method as a Secular Spiritual Practice

The spirit is the conscious ear.
—*EMILY DICKINSON*

Phil, a professional photographer, had been on a religious quest for a decade, which included living for a year at an ashram in India. He frequently spoke of an "unnamed yearning" that dogged him during that time, a part of himself he once knew but had lost. After a Proprioceptive Writing weekend and later a retreat, he wrote to us to say he could now name that yearning: "It's the feeling of being home." He went on: "Other forms of spiritual pursuit simply haven't worked for me—prayer, meditation, yoga. But now I can listen to myself as I write. How exciting to find that my voice speaks so truly when I'm present to hear it."

You may find the greatest benefit of Proprioceptive Writing to be in understanding your emotions or solving problems that develop from habits of perception or misperception. Or you may come to value it most for its spiritual dimension, the way its form and function combine to help you embrace yourself and the world.

Proprioceptive Writing is both a therapy and a meditation. It is part of the humanistic tradition that values the examined life, and it offers a ritualized form for going within. Though it's by no means a substitute for religion, or even related to one, you might take up the practice for some of the same reasons you would join a religion or start a daily meditation practice: out of a wish to establish a new relation to your own thinking so that you do not feel imprisoned or weighed down by it; to lessen your psychological suffering; to find greater clarity of mind; and to develop compassion.

Through the process of focusing your attention and following your thoughts, certain changes invariably occur. Disciplined practice makes you more spontaneous, more inventive, more self-respecting. Your mind becomes calmer, but at the same time, more alert. Your capacity to empathize with others grows and with it your ability to love and forgive. As you engage in your practice, like Phil, you begin to feel at home in yourself.

The ritualistic practices of many religious traditions lead to this same feeling state, though the ways of understanding it may vary. The Christian mystic strives to feel the divine presence of Jesus through contemplative prayer. The meditating Hindu feels such awareness as a merging with Shiva, or Ram, or whichever deity he is meditating upon. At a similar high point in prayer, the Jew or Muslim feels the spirit of God or Allah, although, according to doctrine, he is incapable of embodying divine presence. In this altered state we are removed from our familiar, conditioned ways of thinking and feeling and begin experiencing the joy that comes from being in harmony with ourselves. How liberating it is to say good-bye to guilt and blame.

In this chapter we invite you, regardless of your faith, to experience this mysterious, uplifting side of Proprioceptive Writing, to imagine it as a secular spiritual path whose benefits increase with practice. Let's look more closely at how it does this.

Toby's Story

People often seek out the consolation of a spiritual practice after a life-changing event or tragedy. That was certainly true for me. My mother and father died within two years of each other while I was still a college student in western Pennsylvania, not far from the small town in which I grew up. My older brother, and only sibling, died a few years later. But it was my son, Derek, born with cystic fibrosis when I was twenty-seven, and given a life expectancy—accurate, it turned out—of nine years, who brought death into my life in a way that changed my view of the world. For weeks after I learned about Derek's condition I resisted intimacy with him and its painful reminder of numbered days. But the need to cherish him and nurture his body and mind, as one would a healthy child's, proved irresistible. And so his illness became my teacher, and I resolved to learn from it how to be a loving presence in our brief shared life.

My relationship with my son reached into every corner of my existence. It affected personal choices of every sort: the food I ate, the places I visited, the people I spent time with, the books I read. I was teaching English at Pratt in those days, and many of the students, as well as the other faculty, were exploring existentialism, psychoanalysis, Eastern religions, and mysticism. It was the seventies and experimentation was in the air. I, too, felt compelled to explore a number of these subjects, hoping to find somewhere a conceptual framework that would help me accept the conflicting emotions my son's condition aroused in me.

That year I attended the New York Zendo, where I learned a form of silent, sitting meditation known as *zazen*. A religion of the East, Buddhism flows from an inquiry into the study of mind, making it attractive to Westerners like me whose approach to spirituality is psychologically based. But while Buddhist doctrine addresses thought and thinking, the actual practice of *zazen* involves no engagement of thought. Rather, it achieves its effects by diverting us from thought and its impermanence. As much as I admire the ideas of Zen Buddhism, I felt dissatisfied with its principal ritual, *zazen,* and after a year of practice I gave it up.

For years I thought back on what made this form of meditation wrong for me, but until I established a Proprioceptive Writing practice the answer was not clear. In the *zendo,* expression had a negative value, and stoicism was encouraged. *But I didn't want to suppress my emotions. I wanted to express them!* Often while meditating, beneath my Buddha-like serenity, I was roiling with thoughts and feelings. *Zazen* did not offer me enough chance to let my feelings out.

I was also an English professor and in love with language, although I often felt shy and inexpressive. I wanted to change this about myself. I wanted to speak more, not less. I suspected that until I released my emotions, I could never let go of my thoughts, as one is instructed to do in *zazen*. I sensed that my emotions were locked up in my thoughts, and expressing them through language was key. But in Buddhism, language is not always trusted. Consider the traditional story of an older and younger monk who were walking in the country and came upon a magnificent landscape. "How beautiful this view is," says the younger monk. The old master responds, "Yes, but isn't it a shame you had to say so." The renowned Zen scholar D. T. Suzuki had this to say about the subject: "Zen is not necessarily against words, but it is well aware of the fact that they are always liable to detach themselves from realities and turn into conceptions. And this conceptualization is what Zen is against."

This, then, is one striking difference between Zen meditation and Proprioceptive Writing. In Proprioceptive Writing, rather than let go of our personal thoughts, we engage them, whatever they may be. We write out, test out, and revise thoughts we've lived with for years, which may have ruled our lives. Anything we think during a Write is fair game for expression and reflection. To engage our thoughts actively is a commitment we make when we undertake to do Proprioceptive Writing, a contract we keep with ourselves through regular practice. We do not renegotiate the contract with each new thought that arises—even the most embarrassing and pigheaded thought—but surrender to the process and trust it to liberate us from what Buddhists call "delusions of thought."

Expressing Emotion Through Language

In a Proprioceptive Writing practice, we take for granted the central connection between emotion and the life of the mind. It isn't possible to simply let go of old, unconscious feelings that might be blocking us unless we reach down and grab hold of them. Unexpressed emotion can distort reason and easily leads to a proliferation of false selves. The more shut down I am emotionally, the less experience I'm prompted to think about, and the more resistant I am to change. I become inflexible, stuck in my ways. This inflexibility, although it may make me feel safe, cages me in.

When you practice Proprioceptive Writing, you are doing precisely what the Indian spiritual teacher Krishnamurti asks of us when he responds to a statement with "Let's go into that." You are *going into* your thoughts to find their root in experience, and thereby come to a better understanding of your feelings—an understanding that liberates you from the old, outdated tapes that keep playing in your head.

The truth is that, without writing, it is difficult for most people to go into their thought. By writing you *slow thought down*, find its emotional context in experience, and give yourself the chance to feel its meaning. As E. M. Forster famously asked, "How can I tell what I think till I see what I say?" Writing lets you project your thoughts onto a surface and interact with them. Without writing, you risk losing touch with the thinker in yourself. If you write, you can remember who you are.

For us, this is a spiritual process, because in examining the language of your thought for its associated images and meanings you elevate self-exploration to a form of holy contemplation. Week by week, month by month, you observe the process by which your own mind expands. In turn, you begin to appreciate the inherent potential of all minds to transform. One of the most inspiring sights in the world is a group of proprioceptive writers working side by side in a quiet room, together but alone, protected from intrusion by the intentions of the group, all engaging their thoughts with intensity and openness—like a congregation in prayer.

CREATING RITUAL

All spiritual practices have a focus: breath, postures, the movement of rosaries, the repetition of prayers or sounds, the reading of holy texts. Concentration of mental energies is always the goal. Such concentration cuts through socialized consciousness, for so many a source of pain and suffering, and extends the mind into realms of greater awareness.

When you write proprioceptively, you both create and participate in ritual. As you prepare for a Write, you enter the domain of sacred space and time. You do not rush, and by taking your time, you begin to undo the conditioning that can make you mechanical in thought and feeling. You begin to relax and quiet down, moving away from the everyday world of action and reaction, of getting and spending. For the period of the Write, you are committing yourself to a contemplative mood.

The physical elements of ritual enhance this mood. The candle burning before you helps your concentration, the sounds of Baroque music soothe you, the unlined paper invites you to scribble freely, the closed door shuts out the expectations of others. Even the three breaths you take at the start of the session serve to settle you down in that final moment of centering before the important work begins.

As with many spiritual practices, Proprioceptive Writing makes use of repetition through a mantralike phrase, the Proprioceptive Question. In time it takes root in your thoughts and like every mantra focuses your attention. It leads you from the mundane surface of your words to underlying meanings that connect you with others—one of the basic features of most spiritual paths. When your heart and your head are in sync with each other, you can more readily sense the greater unity of which we are all a part.

LOVING ALONENESS

Most spiritual teachers observe that when you are alone you feel, paradoxically, most connected to the oneness of the world. Proprioceptive Writing makes you comfortable with being alone with your thoughts. Even when you are writing proprioceptively with others, you are alone in their presence, just as you'd be alone in the presence of others if you were meditating in a *zendo*.

Toby describes the situation this way: I know the difficulties of maintaining a solitary meditation practice. When I was a student of Zen, I always found it easier to meditate with others than to sit in my apartment and meditate alone. But I have no difficulty being in solitude when I'm practicing Proprioceptive Writing. I welcome the aloneness. I love to slow down and sink into myself. The Write itself becomes a kind of church, a synagogue, a mosque, and when the music begins, I cross a threshold into sacred space and time that I create myself. The candle, the three breaths, the unlined paper, the uncluttered writing space all seem to anticipate a drama. In that especially beautiful moment just before I put pen to paper, I feel an almost indescribable excitement. I am the conjurer who, through careful listening, can transform ordinary thought into the meaningful information that we explored in the last chapter. I hear my words in the same way I feel my dream imagery, full-bodied and alive, and I am turning up the volume on them without self-consciousness. In the vastness of possibility my solitude offers, I feel like the speaker in William Carlos Williams's poem "Danse Russe," the "happy genius" of my own mind:

If I when my wife is sleeping
and the baby and Kathleen
are sleeping
and the sun is a flame-white disc
in silken mists
above shining trees,—
if I in my north room
dance naked, grotesquely
before my mirror
waving my shirt round my head
and singing softly to myself:
"I am lonely, lonely.
I was born to be lonely,
I am best so!"
If I admire my arms, my face
my shoulders, flanks, buttocks
against the yellow drawn shades,—

Who shall say I am not
the happy genius of my household?

Loving aloneness is one of those hidden gifts of a Proprioceptive Writing practice, like becoming a better reader and a better listener. It's one we hear many people say they are especially grateful for; they're sometimes surprised at the sheer joy and sensual pleasure that solitude offers them during a Write. The subject comes up again and again in people's Writes, though no two individuals describe it in quite the same way. Here's how Irena, a twenty-two-year-old professional gymnast who suffered anxiety attacks, described the solace and freedom from terrifying thoughts that she found in the solitude of her practice.

Why did it take me so long to get here? What was I afraid of? What do I mean by here? *Alone. With myself. In a place of peacefulness and quiet. Surrounded by music. The candlelight flickers. The terror of the day recedes. This is the place I long for, that seems so impossible to get to when I'm in the world. What do I mean by* world? *The noise and the glare, doing my warm-ups, going through my routines, making things happen. It's amazing to enter this place of aloneness yet not feel alone. Emotion rises in me. I'm here! In this great bubble of wonder and ease. What do I mean by* ease? *I have room to feel who I am and to care about the things that matter most to me. It seems I meet myself in a new way. What do I mean by* new? *I feel tenderness for myself. What do I mean by* tenderness? *I forgive myself. I feel calm and still, like a body at rest. The Write is my haven. I find myself here, waiting to be heard. And this is the mystery of it, I can see the high-wire demons and not feel afraid. What do I mean by* demons? *The harsh voices that plague me as I go*

through my day. But in the Write they do not terrify me.
They seem so small. In my Writes I know I am not those
awful thoughts. In the Write I have a safety net beneath
me. I have space. I can breathe.

Divine Ignorance

We'll always remember the look of intense concentration on the faces of the children at Rockport Elementary School in Maine where we taught a modified version of Proprioceptive Writing many years ago. For a week at the beginning of the school day, twenty-eight six- and seven-year-olds made up our class. We explained that we would play some music for them. Because they hadn't yet learned to write, we asked them to "follow" their thoughts by drawing what the music made them think. We had only one rule: During the session they could not call out for attention or interrupt anyone else. Whenever they got fidgety, all it took was a smile from us and a gentle hand gesture to nudge them back to their work, and after a day or two even that wasn't necessary. After the music ended, we stopped at each child's place and asked, "What were you thinking as the music played?" Under each child's drawing we then wrote their responses, which were often poetic. Six-year-old Aaron, for example, told us: "This music feels like New Mexico coming at me!"

We recall that look of rapt, wide-eyed wonder on the faces of those first graders whenever we are trying to communicate to adult students the mental stance to adopt in Proprioceptive

Writing. It's the frame of mind of a child—intent, curious, absorbed. Enter a Write as if you were a child again, fully open to adventure. Find in yourself what some meditation practices call beginner's mind. Take each word you hear as if it were new, without assuming to know what it means. Write in the spirit of what American mystic Adi Da has called "divine ignorance" and remember our directive from Chapter 2—receive, receive, receive. Or recall Jesus' admonition to the apostles: To understand his word, we must become "like little children," guileless and without pretense.

Over time, Proprioceptive Writing helps you to develop a sense of *negative capability*, a trait the poet John Keats described as the capacity to exist in "uncertainties, mysteries, doubts, without any irritable reaching after fact and reason," a quality he felt was indispensable to achievement in literature. Musician and scientist Manfred Clynes, in his book *Sentics: The Touch of the Emotions*, uses yet another term to describe this kind of undefended receptivity: *being apreene.* When someone is apreene, says Clynes, he or she exists in a state of "eager expectancy . . . which includes an intellectual ardor and openness. . . . This emotion is accompanied by a sense of lightness and quiet in the body, the absence of anxiety, and trust that ideas received will be worthy." These are the very qualities we witnessed in those first graders. And indeed, without such trust, the door to expression slams shut, and the gatekeeper, or inner critic as we sometimes call it, maintains dominion over our creative natures. Through Proprioceptive Writing, you can practice negative capability and learn to be apreene.

If you can hold yourself in this state while in a Write, open and accepting of whatever comes to you, you can begin to undo habituated responses to thought, the kind of automatic reactions you've developed over the years and may not even realize you're having. As a listener, you become attuned to yourself, both when you're practicing Proprioceptive Writing and when you're not.

LISTENING WITHOUT BIAS

One summer when our seven-year-old nephew was vacationing with us in Maine, he jumped into low water from a very high pier and twisted his ankle. Later, when we were driving home from the hospital, relieved that he hadn't broken anything, we asked if he hadn't heard a voice inside himself warning him not to jump. He said yes, but it was so soft he'd hardly heard it.

Not only are our inner thoughts quiet, but we hear them through filters, or what British psychiatrist R. D. Laing called "social trance." Laing once said that we are first hypnotized by our society, and then further hypnotized into believing we haven't been hypnotized! This degree of unawareness can't be undone in a weekend workshop; it requires a regular home practice. In Proprioceptive Writing, you're listening not just to your individual thoughts but to their connectedness, without judgment or bias. You listen to the words through which thought speaks to you and become apreene to the truths they carry.

Let's overhear someone in this state of unbiased listening, in the flowing, receptive mode we're talking about. This is part of an early Write of a florist named Sookie. Watch her capacity for surprise, as the world of certainty gives way to mystery and the creative space of not knowing.

Just out of the shower. Thinking madly of where to start today. Why is this where-to-start business so important? Is this the me that is trying to handle Proprioceptive Writing? What do I mean by handle? *Control. Have some power over, make it easier for myself. I just can't wait to stop fighting PW. What do I mean by* fighting? *Holding myself against it in some way. Not letting the process take me where it wants, and what do I mean by the* process? *It is the means by which my mind reveals itself in all of its clarity and confusion. It is the process of growing up, of growing. What do I mean by* growing? *To get bigger. To get as big as you can. To expand forever. What a thought! I have this picture of me in the universe like a giant morning glory vine, just going everywhere. What do I mean by* everywhere? *Unknown places and crevices. Are we ever-expanding or are we pulsating, up and down, back and forth, in and out? My mind feels like a dancer. What do I mean by* dancer? *A mover and shaker. There must be some force that drives us to move, change, mature, know. What do I mean by* know? *The word suddenly sounds peculiar. What do I know? I know that I am sitting here wondering if I know anything. I am sit-*

ting here knowing that as I write something the act of writing changes it, it shifts before my very eyes. Like a dancer with veils.

What thoughts were heard but not written? *None. I feel like I got everything except for a description of the dance.*

How do I feel now? *Tingling, full of life, ready to change my activity and get to work.*

What larger story is the Write part of? *I think it's about not knowing or maybe something about the mystery of knowing.*

What ideas came up for future Writes? *Pay attention to how things change in a Write.*

What is noteworthy about Sookie's Write is how she, like any Zen master, lets her thoughts flow without judging them. She is relaxed, fluid, and apreene as her associations shift and change. At the beginning of the Write, Sookie is scattered ("thinking madly" of where to begin her day). By the end, her direction is clear. Her Write demonstrates that Proprioceptive Writing is not only relaxing and stress-reducing but spiritually energizing. Listening without prejudice, identifying with the process of her thinking rather than with the thoughts themselves, produces in Sookie the kind of energy common to such dancing sects as Shakers, Hassids, and Whirling Dervishes.

TRANSFORMATIVE UNDERSTANDING

As we said earlier, Proprioceptive Writing is a ritualized practice that celebrates the examined life. It is exemplified by the Zen story of the prisoner who is set free but is still in his open cell the next day when the jailer comes by. When asked why, the prisoner replies, "I know I'm free to go, but what I need to understand is, how did I get here in the first place?"

A simple joy comes to you whenever you feel understood by another or feel that you understand another. An even sweeter, more lasting pleasure infuses you when you gain understanding of your own understandings—about yourself or others—the wisdom the prisoner in the Zen story was seeking. All proprioceptive writers know the delight of discovering new meaning in an old story after realizing something about themselves that they didn't know before, then telling the story differently. When old understandings expand into new comprehension, you sense a movement that is invigorating and feels awesome. As you leap from the narrower viewpoint to the broader, as persuaded now by the latter as you once were by the former, you realize that in your life, as in the world, nothing is permanently fixed.

A learning experience like this transforms you, alters you at the roots. It makes you question who you are and what you know. Saul becomes Paul; Jacob becomes Israel. You are not the same! When you contemplate your thoughts in writing, gaining proprioceptive information in the process, dead thought cracks off and falls away. New thought takes its place. You are altered, deeply and permanently.

If this expansion of understanding occurs with sufficient frequency, you experience this movement as growth on a spiritual path. There is no limit to the mind's ability to expand in this way. This is why, when Zen master Ado Roshi was once asked if you stop meditating upon reaching spiritual enlightenment, he roared, "No! No! More! More! Deeper! Deeper!" In other words, it is the nature of the mind to grow by constantly incorporating old understandings into new, larger ones. Practiced regularly, the Proprioceptive Writing process keeps you in touch with this spiritual adventure.

A PATH TO FORGIVENESS

According to reports presented at a Harvard Medical School conference on "Spirituality in Healing," held in Chicago in March 1999 under the direction of Herbert Benson, physician and author of *The Relaxation Response*, the theme that dominates the minds of those who are dying is that they be forgiven. As we all know, forgiveness isn't just a deathbed issue; the need to forgive and be forgiven is profoundly and universally human. Every major world religion has a ritual or sacrament, such as confession, or a holiday, such as Yom Kippur, to relieve its practitioners of guilt for real or imagined wrongdoing. Years ago Alan Watts speculated that freedom from guilt might even be the Western equivalent of Eastern spiritual liberation.

We believe it is through transformative understanding—the kind that produces lasting change—that the liberating act of forgiveness occurs. You can't forgive yourself or anyone else in a genuine, honest-to-God way if you don't comprehend something in a new way; at most you may succeed in forgetting. Such leaps in understanding happen regularly in Proprioceptive Writing every time you gain proprioceptive information; in these moments, as you sit back and take yourself in, you feel in your heart what you think with your mind. Suddenly, when you know something about yourself and others that includes and exceeds what you knew formerly, gratitude is upon you, like grace, for the wisdom you've gained. On its heels comes compassion—the there-but-for-the-grace-of-God-go-I feeling—the opening volley of forgiveness.

We're reminded of a story that is unique in its details but typical of the spiritual growth that occurs in Proprioceptive Writing. In her late fifties, a longtime student of ours named Roberta suddenly developed a passion for studying Yiddish, the language her late mother had spoken in her childhood home. She began taking Yiddish language lessons, listening to Yiddish music and songs, reading Yiddish literature, all of which reawakened her memories of her mother. Their relationship had always been difficult. Roberta had grown up convinced her mother was cruel and she herself was unlovable, a belief that lingered long past her mother's death. As evidence of this, Roberta often told the story of having been "force-fed" by her mother as a child. In the final Write of our workshop, Roberta again drifted into an imagining of one of these feeding scenes. But this time she gained proprioceptive information from it and so experienced the event differently. She heard her mother's pleading, demanding voice as she fed her, but now, for the first time, Roberta's hearing was informed by the plaintive tones of Yiddish, her mother's first language, with the history of fear and deprivation it carried. What she sensed now was a mother's desperate concern for her daughter's health and survival. How she wept as she read her Write! All at once she felt cradled and cared for, rather than attacked by those words. She had been loved all along. With tears flowing copiously, Roberta forgave herself for a lifetime of resentment and forgave her mother her limitations as well. Compassion bloomed in her.

Roberta's story illustrates the way forgiveness can follow from an expanded perception of a primal experience. It is an important story for another reason. We have heard hundreds of Writes in which the dominant theme is the relationship to the mother. We've worked with people in their seventies and even into their eighties for whom the mother story is still being resolved. Although these relationships may be excruciatingly complex, we've often thought that if people could manage to forgive their mothers, the world would magically transform into a place of love. As it was for Roberta, Proprioceptive Writing can provide a means for handling this profoundly rewarding spiritual work.

If you are angry or resentful or feel punishing toward a mother or a father, or anyone who has wounded you in the past, it's likely that those feelings will come up in a Write. This is your opportunity to examine them—not eradicate them, but revisit the experience that produced them. Reliving those events in the tranquillity of the Write may make it possible to outgrow a hurt. Without that hurt feeling you may see the parent in a new light.

COMPASSION AND GUILT

It isn't possible to have compassion for another without feeling it for yourself. This is the assumption behind the biblical teaching to "love thy neighbor as thyself" and is a premise of all religions. The capacity for compassion is born and nurtured by the inner experience of movement, what we've described as transformative understanding. Who were you before you became who you are now? Can you remember how you thought yesterday, or ten years ago, without hostility or pride, but merely as an expression of becoming the person you are? Can you accept that attitudes tomorrow may conflict with today's? Is it possible to suspend judgment momentarily and imagine yourself other than as you are now? As you become more reflective you can remember in an increasingly thoughtful way how you once felt and recall in a feeling way how you once thought. This proprioceptive memory of yourself in your many forms and guises enables you to find within yourself the source of empathy with the other.

The following Write belongs to John, a Baptist preacher from South Carolina. Now nearly seventy, he had turned recently to sculpture as a medium of expression. His work had found its way into several folk-art collections. Yet, as you will

hear, he suffered mightily from guilt and regret for anger harbored all his life toward his father, and for the grief his rage had
caused his own daughter, Latisha. But the greatest guilt he re-
served for himself—for polluting his life with resentment
toward his father now many years dead. Until this Write, he
told us later, he felt helpless to change or to forgive himself.

John begins to speak here about the effect his bitterness had
on him, and in doing so, reaches a turning point that affects not
only his lifelong battle with anger but also his art. He feels for
the little boy who trembled with fear when confronted by his
father, but also feels the price he paid for his enduring rage, the
suffering he caused himself and those he loves. In the course of
this Write he imagines a serene father and, in this way, grows
beyond the damage of that relationship.

*I am picturing the head of my father for a new sculpture.
I want to make it serene—a large serene head of ebony.
What do I mean by* serene head? *I cannot say without
hearing what the voice of chaos speaks. What do I mean
by the* voice of chaos? *The voice I've heard these sixty-
nine years. The voice of fear, the voice of my mother's
tears, the silent anguish falling with her tears into the
dishwater, the voice of my father's anguished rage before
which we all trembled, the voice of my sister's suffering
silence, my brother's sigh of resignation. What do I mean
by* resignation? *I mean I resign from life. I turn away
from God and settle for the fear and rage I feel bubbling*

inside me. What do I mean by inside me? *I mean I am the rage, the unlovedness, the diabolical self-pity. What did I give up? I gave up my hope that I was love. What do I mean by* love? *I mean the hope that I have within me, a positive power that infuses me, that oozes from my pores, uncontrolled, unaccountable, indescribable.*

Now, now I am on the verge of seeing the serene head. I must give up that sense of hatred, that poor me, that victim of powers outside myself, and in its place comes compassion for my "persecutors." What do I mean by persecutors? *I mean my angry father. Instead to see him as a frightened man who was lost, drowning in his hatred of himself. Now I feel a warmth for him I could never have believed possible when I was cowering in fear and hatred of him. So it's now I can have compassion also for Latisha, who still hates the memory of my hatred, my chaos-filled rage and who thus hates the image of me, as if I am still that now. Now I can open my heart to her without fear of the awful hell of guilt, I can live at last by the Golden Rule.*

The open heart returns to look upon the hate with love. What do I mean by love? *I mean the fearlessness of being, a sureness of a solid base, a presence immovable, an unchangeably benign presence, untouchable to all the hates.*

There, there is the serene head emerging. See! It grows from the unformed fibers of the wood. Oh see its beauty! Feel the sweet texture. Smell the peaceful odor of its essence. The cries of chaos, the spearpoint of contempt, the roils of vengeance—all are lost to my awareness in the blessed moment. This is the serene head.

I will carve this head as the head I wished for my father, the head I still wish for him. I offer it to him as a gift to his memory and to make him me, to end the memory of separation from him. I feel the tears now. What I always wanted to do, embrace him and feel the surging bond between us that I never knew was there. The serene head—I'll carve it as a gift to him.

The "voice of chaos" is John's term for the memories of family misery that are buried within him. He cannot develop spiritually, or visualize the serene image of his father that he desires to sculpt, without first expressing how these memories feel to him—and this he does, poetically, in the tranquillity of the Write. The "voice of chaos" feels like fear itself, like a mother's tears at the sink, like anguish in a father's rage, like a silently suffering sister, like a brother's sigh of resignation.

What John expresses through his own voice he can hear, and what he can hear he can feel. Hearing, then, awakens John to himself. He sees the young boy he once was, a force for love and hope, and at the same time sees the tormented soul that boy became. Overcome with emotion, he experiences his own loss, which frees him to feel for others. By invoking the Golden Rule—"do unto others as you would have others do unto you"—he expresses compassion for his daughter's suffering now that he has forgiven his father and recognized himself as a force for love.

Max's Awakening

Max was an undergraduate who had been in Toby's introductory literature class. At that time, Toby was using Proprioceptive Writing in the classroom to spur students to think in new directions, to discover themes and connections between the literature they were reading and their own lives.

At the beginning of the semester Max sat glumly in the back of the classroom in a pair of sweatpants and a sweatshirt, like a quarterback who'd just blown the big game. Although his assignments were handed in on time, his work was mechanical. Here's a portion of the Write Max submitted after Toby asked the students to explore their thinking on any subject they chose:

> *What basically is a lawyer? Well, he is a person just like you and me; whether you call him or her an attorney, counselor, esquire, counsel, barrister, or solicitor, a lawyer is a person authorized to practice law. Contrary to popular belief, most lawyers rarely go to court. Perry Mason is not your typical lawyer. The practice of law usually involves giving advice, preparing legal papers, or arguing something for somebody else—all for a fee. . . .*

And so on. Max's writing showed that he was quite capable of reporting information and repeating facts from something he'd read. He just couldn't bring *himself* into his writing. When it came to expressing his own thoughts or feelings about what truly interested him, confused him, or touched him in a personal way in what he was reading, he kept coming up empty. Not only was Max's writing mechanical, he never volunteered an opinion in class. He acted cut off and bored.

Since Max wouldn't speak up or express unguarded thought in his Writes, Toby decided to write questions to him that Max could reflect on in writing. One day Toby presented him with the question, Why am I afraid to think? Max's writing became deeper and more reflective from that point on.

> *Why am I afraid to think? Maybe I'm afraid I'm making a fool of myself and that all the others here are so much better at your method. Or maybe it makes me feel lonely to be on my own, without radio or TV. Maybe what I think seems weird. But a funny thing happened to me yesterday. I was writing and whatever thoughts came up to me I looked back at, then I was not alone and not lonely. This was the first time this had ever happened. . . .*

In *Walden*, Thoreau says that even if he were a prisoner in an attic, he would be a free man as long as he was able to think. Max was beginning to experience for himself a state of mind like Thoreau's. From this Write forward Max was a changed person. He became more personal, self-expressive, and insightful, not just in his writing but in his class interactions as well. The freedom of the form and the self-trust he was developing allowed him to show the intelligence he had been concealing, even from himself. In subsequent Writes, he continued to mend his proprioceptive disconnection. In his final Write Max tells a spiritual awakening story, thus ending the course where some students begin it: with the recognition of the thinker in himself as divine. Listen to how he recounts the experience that took place almost a decade earlier.

On a dark afternoon—I was ten or eleven—I was walk-ing on a country road. On my left, a patch of curly kale; on my right, some yellow Brussels sprouts. I felt a snowflake on my cheek, and from far away in the charcoal-gray sky I saw the slow approach of a snow-storm. I stood still; some flakes were now falling around my feet. A few melted on the ground, others stayed intact. Then I heard the falling of the snow, with the softest hiss-ing sound. I stood transfixed, listening, and knew what can never be expressed—that the natural is supernatural and that I am the eye that hears and the ear that sees, that what is outside me happens in me, that outside and inside are one. . . . Is this so different from the divine in man, or from what is meant by the spirit?

Later, Max described this Write as "a portrait of a young man as a mystic," and said that the image of this scene had lived with him for ten years, but he had only become aware of it in this Write. He spoke to the class about his shift in mood as he focused on the snowflakes and how they felt on his skin. In the course of the Write, he said, a calm suffused him; the world seemed safe; he felt awakened and empowered.

This heightened consciousness was a direct result of the interplay of thought and emotion in Proprioceptive Writing. While hiding in the back of the classroom, Max was unaware of his powers as a thinking, feeling person. He'd had intimations of a religious or mystical sensibility before, but until this Write it remained unrealized.

Sometimes, like Max, we enter that quiet moment just before a Write with anxiety, afraid we'll find nothing, neither substance nor energy. But as the music plays, as the candle burns, as our minds find their focus in our thoughts, a point of view shifts, a new story emerges, and we realize again that our practice is a life raft. The more we explore, the more we discover; it is impossible for us to run dry. We see before us on the page and feel within us a process unfolding, orderly and vital. We remember ourselves again, and the pleasure of that surprise feels magical. We open our minds and the world opens before us.

Chapter Six

Creating a
Lifelong Practice

Practice is the best of all instructors.
—*PUBLIUS SYRUS*

Now that you know the basics of how to do a Write, and what benefits it can have for you, you'll need to maintain your practice after the novelty's worn off. In certain ways, Proprioceptive Writing resembles other rituals, like yoga or meditation, journaling or writing "morning pages," or even physical exercise, like jogging or swimming. The more frequently you do them, the more effective they are. But you'll have good days and bad days. Not every meditation session leads to blissful enlightenment. Some days you feel terrific after a jog, other days you feel as if you've been hit by a truck. Likewise, not every Proprioceptive Writing session will leave you irresistibly energized or produce profound insights about the ways of the world, but some will.

In this chapter, we'll share with you techniques for deepening and sustaining your individual practice over the long haul. We'll also talk about doing Proprioceptive Writing in groups, with a partner, or with your family.

THE GUIDED WRITE

When people are just beginning to do Proprioceptive Writing, we tell them not to start out with an agenda. It's important to become accustomed to leaving yourself open to whatever comes into your mind, even though that openness feels risky at first. Being totally open and attentive to spontaneous thought is good training for the kind of listening you'll do in your practice. Get used to looking down at that perfectly white page before you, and let it pull you into your current thought stream, whatever that may be. Learn to "make a middle"—that is, don't worry about finding a good beginning for the Write. Simply take the first thought that presents itself and begin. We recommend you work this way for the first three months.

After that time, when you're starting to feel more at home with the form—you feel your mental muscles strengthening and gaining more flexibility—you might want to have what we call a guided Write, which begins with a clear agenda, a question you wish to answer, or an issue you want to get to the bottom of. Used in this way, the Write becomes a kind of problem-solving project. One of our former students, a graphic designer named Spencer, wrote to us recently to tell us about a string of professional successes he was having in advertising, most of which he attributed to using guided Writes to think through design issues. Here's how he got started in one of the Writes he sent us:

> *I've got to come up with an idea for Becky's handwoven rugs. Everyone loves them—their fabulous texture, their vibrant colors—but how to bring this out in the brochure? What do I mean by* vibrant? *They're so vivid, they seem to lift off the floor. What do I mean by* lift off? *Like a magic carpet. Like, maybe an image of Becky sitting on one of her rugs, floating above her studio. All right, there's an idea I can go with. But her studio itself is so cool, I'd also like to show her actually weaving. Okay, maybe a series of shots, beginning with . . .*

How can you tell what topics might make good fodder for a guided Write? Take careful note of your answers to the fourth question: "What ideas came up for future Writes?" You might even want to run a highlighting pen over your answers. Once a month, or whenever you're looking for some direction in your practice, look through what you've highlighted for something that speaks to you now. Or, you can use a notebook and simply jot down your answers and never refer to your finished Writes again.

One caution: Don't lock yourself into an agenda just because you started with it. Let your thoughts go where they want to and listen to them. If you keep your mind on the process you're engaged in (writing what you hear, listening to what you write, being ready to ask the PQ), the content will take care of itself. The goal is not a shapely essay on a topic but simply to explore something that's on your mind, something you're curious about, or something that is troubling you. The art of handling a guided Write is to be sensitive enough to know when the material that emerges is showing you another path to take, one that may not, on the surface at least, have anything to do with your proposed agenda. If you follow the seemingly unrelated path, you may discover the answer you were after.

THE FILING SYSTEM OF THE MIND

Another way to extend and deepen your practice is to begin organizing your Writes into files that distinguish recurring themes in your life. Like us, we think you'll be continually surprised at how clearly the process of Proprioceptive Writing displays them: sometimes you're not even aware of these themes until you write down the answer to the question "What larger story is the Write part of?" Though Writes don't necessarily focus squarely on any particular topic, you can often sense a theme running beneath them like a current. Revisiting certain scenes and thoughts in your Writes enables you to learn from them. Grouping your Writes according to subject helps you see your progress. You feel smarter as your stories gain complexity.

Although everyone has innumerable thoughts, we've observed over the years that they fall into categories, among them are the following:

The Culture/Society Story. Stories of experience, attitudes and feelings involving race, gender, religion, ethnicity, culture, and country. Tension between autonomy and community. Stories of political conviction or alienation from politics.

The Family Story. We've touched on the centrality of the mother story in our lives. But there is also the father story, the sibling story, the only child story, the grandparent story, the orphan story, the adoption story, the divorce story, the marriage story, the in-law story, the stepparent story.

The Relationship Story. Stories of short- or long-term, casual or intense relationships with friends, lovers, partners past and present, teachers, colleagues, employers or employees, neighbors, even cherished animals.

The Money/Class Story. Stories connected to wealth or lack of it, social standing, past and present, and the feelings associated with them. These are among the most taboo subjects in our collective psyche, despite the fact that money is on everyone's mind.

The Work Story. Stories about the work you do, or dream of doing. Attitudes toward ambition, creative work, intellectually stimulating work, service. Issues of power and entitlement at work; of being overworked, overlooked;

of perfectionism. Questions about what constitutes legitimate work. Feelings of imbalance between your work and your personal life.

The Aging Story. Life's stages, the sense of time passing, diminishing or growing empowerment.

The Death and Dying Story. Stories about loss, threat of loss, and ambivalence toward life. Fears, anxieties, and other feelings that emerge from our knowledge that we are going to die.

The Emotions Story. Stories that come up in connection to the emotions of love, hate, envy, fury, grief, reverence, joy, shame, awe, pity, despair, guilt, greed, sexual passion, jealousy. Be prepared to name new emotional states as you observe or experience them, and combinations of states that may be perplexing, such as grief/shame, anger/sadness, love/hate.

The Learning Story. The shaping power of education on development, both in and out of school.

The Sex Story. Stories about feelings connected to your body—your femaleness or maleness; attitudes about sexual desire, preferences, and experience.

Of course, any given story might be observed through the lens of different categories. How you choose to name and file your Writes is up to you. Some of our students collect the Writes they've accumulated in a particular area and bind them in a unique or artistic way, with the intention of leaving them to family or friends. Not that their writing constitutes a literary work, but it is a personal document reflecting their sense of themselves.

Sacred Study: The Proprioceptive Writing Study Session

The study session Toby developed for Proprioceptive Writing students consists of a series of activities that can greatly enrich your understanding of a particular Write or group of Writes. Virtually everything in a Write is fair game for reflection: the words you are using, your concepts, your opinions, your beliefs, your feelings, your conjectures, your attitudes, your memories. At its best, studying a Write means using it as a text that contains important information rather than viewing it passively. We call this study sacred out of reverence for a process in which all questions are valid and desirable.

The idea is to consider previously written Writes, but also to allow yourself to generate new material that comes naturally as you engage in the activity.

To prepare for a study session, use the rituals you would for an ordinary Write. You should be alone, in a place where you will not be disturbed for at least thirty minutes, and have a stack of unlined white paper in front of you, as well as the Write or Writes you want to explore. Use any (wordless) music that relaxes and focuses you. In addition to a candle and music, have on the table paints, crayons, colored pencils, and the like.

Enter the session in the spirit in which you ordinarily enter

a Write. Be apreene, open to adventure and possibility, and prepared to surrender completely to your impulses. In the half
hour (or more) session you've arranged for, do one or more of
the following activities:

- Read all or part of the group of Writes (even one).
- Write, if you feel moved. Feel free to riff off of any words,
  phrases, or sentences of the text.
- Mark or color-code any parts you wish to either study further or copy out for use later.
- List the sequence of PQs in a particular Write or series of
  Writes. Does a story reveal itself?
- List the people who show up in a Write, and reflect on
  your shared history.
- Explore your Writes for their metaphors. Do they tell a
  story? (One student who did this discovered that almost all
  the metaphors in the Writes in her The Husband Story file
  were of war and battle. This helped her understand why
  she was feeling so defeated in her marriage.)
- List and/or draw the visual images in the Write.
- List those words you would like to explore proprioceptively but didn't get to when you first wrote them.
- Take note of those statements in a Write that seem to
  contain important truths. Copy them into a separate notebook or write them on cards and begin quoting yourself.
- As you explore the Writes, be open to creating other activities that might enhance your next study session. For
  example, note or sketch out ideas for writing projects if

you're interested in formal writing. Or ask yourself the four questions, but pertaining to the study session rather than an individual Write.

To get the most out of study sessions, be very flexible within them. For instance, if you've highlighted a passage in a Write from three months ago, and you spend the remainder of the session writing about it, so be it. If you've stumbled on a visual image that excites you and you take a half hour to draw your feelings rather than write them, that's okay. Feel free to move back and forth between old Writes and the new ideas and thoughts they generate. Be especially attentive in this back-and-forth movement to your common subject matter. For example, let's say you've been reflecting on a highlighted section of an old Write about anger and it takes you to a new thought about your sister, which you write out. You then go back to the original Write you were just exploring and read the part that *wasn't* highlighted, and you find that that section, too, involved a story about your sister. When this happens—and it happens frequently—you'll experience a harmonious feeling, as if all the dots, for the moment, seem to connect.

WORKING WITH GROUPS

Perhaps the greatest aid to supporting your Proprioceptive Writing practice is writing with another person or in a group. We know students who make an appointment to write at the same time, then read their Writes to each other over the phone. It is enormously helpful, as you create a long-term practice, to hear other people's Writes, if only to gain a feel for what is possible, to understand how much freedom there is in the form. This is why the group Write can inspire and strengthen your own individual work.

In this section we offer some guidelines to working successfully with others, including how to choose participants, the proper structure for a group session, how to give and receive feedback, and issues of confidentiality.

THE PARTICIPANTS

We often think of proprioceptive writers as itinerant musicians looking for an opportunity to get together and jam. Theoretically, any person who has taken an introductory Proprioceptive Writing course with a certified teacher, or has read this book and begun his or her own practice, should be eligible to participate in a Proprioceptive Writing group. The vast majority of the workshops we run, for example, have no special requirements of its members—we get people from their twenties to their eighties, male and female, on every possible career path, and of diverse ethnic and religious backgrounds. We like the mix of voices this kind of open grouping creates. But occasionally we also organize sessions for groups that want to focus on particular needs. Linda leads workshops for writers, psychotherapists, ministers, and other special interest groups, while Toby, a poet, runs poetry workshops, using Writes for inspiration, and Proprioceptive Writing groups for men. These specialized group sessions are no less likely than heterogeneous ones to produce diverse and surprising thought in writing.

For your own reasons, you may prefer to take part in a Proprioceptive Writing group exclusively of women or men, or of writers or artists (though make sure it doesn't evolve into a "craft" workshop, where work is critiqued for revision). Some groups are closed, some welcome newcomers. In any case, it is a commitment to work within the parameters of the guidelines described here that is essential.

HOSTING A PROPRIOCEPTIVE WRITING GROUP SESSION

Most groups meet anywhere from once a week to once a month, depending on the wishes of the group members. Some groups meet at the same person's home every time, others rotate among members' homes. Without a teacher present, it is the host who sets the tone, is responsible for assuring the group's total privacy, and ensures the smooth functioning of the session. The host takes care of the music, and provides the candles, paper, pens or pencils, and stapler. We do not recommend the usual process of going around in a circle for introductions, even when members are meeting for the first time; instead, we ask participants to say their names before reading their Write. If the host serves snacks, they should be available before and after, not during, a Write.

Once people have greeted one another and settled down, it's time to begin turning inward. Remember, material is seeking expression in you, and for it to come to the surface, you need quietude, receptivity, and attentiveness. As we've said in earlier chapters, the moments just before the Write begins are some of the most beautiful in the Proprioceptive Writing ritual, when the group feels its common intent and prepares itself to write. The host, or person in charge of the music, should not rush this moment or use the music to quiet the group. Rather, wait until the group is completely silent.

In a group, when the writing period is over, participants have the opportunity to read their Writes aloud. But before the reading begins, people may want to snack or stretch or socialize a bit. Generally, keep breaks short and don't begin reading until the group has the same sense of focus as it had during the Write itself. If it seems needed, the host can sound a chime to indicate that it's now time for the reading.

READING ALOUD, LISTENING, AND GIVING FEEDBACK

We sometimes tell students to read their Writes aloud as if written by someone else. This gives them a little distance from the material, so they can hear it as a reader rather than as a writer might. Likewise, we advise students to listen to other people's Writes as if they themselves had written them. This helps them attend to the group's members with interest and imagination.

Always read to discover, never to impress or entertain. Read slowly enough to take in your words; read loudly enough for everyone to hear you without straining, but don't make a studied performance of it. Remember, you do not have to defend your Write, or even like it particularly. The Write is its own world, like a dream, and you are not responsible for it. You do not have to account for yourself. You may hold positions that conflict with those you express in the Write; you may be inconsistent. Situations you describe may have layers of complexity you have not addressed. All this is understood. Even though the group setting increases the stakes, all you have to do now is hear what you have written.

Pause for a moment between readings. Don't rush from person to person. If you don't go around in a circle but volunteer to read when you feel ready, serendipitous patterns may emerge.

Most Proprioceptive Writing groups allow feedback either after each reading or when everyone has finished. There's no set rule here. But *how* participants respond to the Writes of others, in word and spirit, does have rules, because mistakes here have serious consequences. It is absolutely crucial that the people working together understand and respect certain boundaries in relation to hearing, giving, and receiving feedback. Most important, you must understand that the person reading will not be well served by offers of help, advice, guidance, or, for that matter, even compliments. The fact is, expressed judgments of any sort, *including those implied by encouragement and praise,* divert the entire group from its purpose.

Here is one example of the harm that can be done. A few years ago, Barbara, a former student, joined an ad hoc Proprioceptive Writing group near her home in Pennsylvania. She was a professional playwright who had just begun her first novel. Each time she read aloud, several other group members commented on how much they loved her writing style. Even her Writes could surely be published, they told her. But Barbara had joined the Proprioceptive Writing group specifically to get away from having her work judged, as it was in regular writing groups. She wanted to be free to write whatever she was thinking and feeling and not worry about what anyone else thought of it. Some group members introduced their readings by apologizing for their inadequate prose, which showed that they were using their writing to the wrong purpose. Something important had been lost. Although Barbara's enthusiastic listeners meant no harm, they were taking her off her chosen course, and confusing other members about the goals of a Proprioceptive Writing group.

While you're listening to someone's Write, take notes and use them if you choose to give feedback. But don't feel compelled to respond. If you do respond, stay as close to the Write as possible. Make no assumptions that the Write does not invite you to make, and do not judge its content. As a general rule, extemporize very little. Something in another's Write may strike you powerfully, or raise questions for you. Something someone says may remind you of yourself. The point of feedback is not critique but information about yourself. Some groups forgo the feedback phase altogether, especially if the group is large and time is limited or if the members so decide. This choice is perfectly reasonable and may even be preferable.

How should you respond to feedback? Ideally with silence. Don't defend or explain yourself. If you are left with unresolved issues or are feeling uncomfortable because of something that was said, think of the experience as material for more writing. If you feel hurt or misunderstood by the feedback, or if you needed feedback you didn't get, plow these feelings into another Write. Don't try to work out your reactions directly with the other participants. That is not the purpose of the group.

CONFIDENTIALITY

The Proprioceptive Writing group session is an intimate event. While participating in one, you are privy to information, thoughts, and feelings that may never have been expressed by the writer before, may never be expressed again elsewhere, and may even come as a surprise to the person writing them. For these reasons it is of utmost importance that proprioceptive writers respect each other's privacy and never discuss a Write with an outside party. Even within the group, for example, during a break, do not refer to the contents of another person's Write casually, or ask further questions about it without being invited to do so. Every Write, though not secret, is confidential and belongs to the writer alone.

OPENINGS AND CLOSINGS

Though intimate, a Proprioceptive Writing group is not a social group. It is a writing and listening group. Whether you are writing, reading your Write aloud, hearing another's Write, or receiving or giving feedback, active listening is your goal. To make a comfortable transition into and out of this friendly but nonsocial atmosphere, it helps to indicate the opening and closing of the session in some formal manner. You might use a simple gesture to gather the group: sound a chime or a gong or ring a bell. Similarly, after the Writes have been read and the session is over, you might stand in a silent circle for a minute or two. This brief ritual honors your work and signifies the transition back into the everyday world.

Frequently Asked Questions About Proprioceptive Writing Groups

If the Proprioceptive Writing group is leaderless and something goes awry, what's to be done? How should the group handle problems that arise?

Immediately before the Write begins, the host might ask if there is any "old business" before the group. If there is none, move directly into the Write. But anyone who wishes to address a problem of protocol should do so. If you feel there has been too much socializing during previous sessions, for example, especially between readings, or if the feedback exchange has become judgmental or interpretive, observe this fact in a general way and, if you wish, refer to this book or to Proprioceptive Writing teachers for guidance. Having the courage to take the procedures seriously will help the group stay on course and pay off in the end.

Should I avoid writing about people in the group, even if I think of them during the Write?

This depends entirely on the members of the group. If you're concerned with this question, others may be, too. You might try having a guided Write on the subject and decide to-gether what you want to do about it.

What happens if a reader is overcome by emotion?

Give the reader time and space to experience the strong feelings before moving on to the next reader. We've found that people usually appreciate the chance the group gives them to let their emotions be fully expressed. After a while their feelings usually subside, and they can indicate by a nod that they're ready to listen to the next reader. Don't assume that people need to be rescued from their emotions, or comforted by gestures of concern. Though you may have the best intentions at heart, your overeagerness to console a reader, either during or follow-ing a session, can make that person feel exposed and uncomfort-able. As one student wrote to us in a letter after a workshop: "The guidelines about boundaries gave me a sense of respect for others in the group and for myself, a sense of permission that was a new experience. It completely changed the meaning of in-timacy for me."

COUPLES WRITING TOGETHER

You will often feel a sense of intimacy with the person reading a Write aloud. This is not due simply to its content. When some-one lets you in on his or her thinking, the bond between you is strengthened. You glimpse what it's like to be that person. For this reason, we often hear proprioceptive writers claim to know the people they write with better than anyone else in their lives, and feel better known by the people they write with than by anyone else. If such empathy springs up among strangers, think what a boon it can be for a couple!

Simply listening to your partner, in the way you learn to listen proprioceptively, can have a deeply nourishing effect on your relationship. For that half hour or so, you're not focused on the kids, the bills, the tiling in the bathroom that's crumbling; you're not thinking of your everyday responsibilities and burdens. You're there to follow your thoughts in each other's presence. And when your partner listens to your thoughts with the attention of a Proprioceptive Writing listener, you feel known by the person you love.

The work you do with Proprioceptive Writing always starts with yourself, then generates understanding outward. The more we reveal ourselves to ourselves, the more we can reveal ourselves to another. The more we reveal ourselves to another, the more fully we are individuated from each other, and the less prone we are to project feelings onto each other. The result of this process is a more satisfying connection: centered in myself, I don't fear losing myself in you; centered in yourself, you likewise have less fear of losing yourself in me. We can both *be* and *be in relationship with* at the same time.

We've asked couples for their thoughts about the effect Proprioceptive Writing had on their relationships. The responses of Isabel and Maurice, who married a mere month after they met, are representative. Isabel told us that since starting to practice Proprioceptive Writing together, she knows Maurice better. "When I listen to Maurice read one of his Writes, I hear him at his most interesting. There are facets of him I never saw before, which gives me a greater feeling of possibility for him and for us. Increasingly, I see him as a person with romantic yearnings rather than as someone bounded by home and job. And as he reveals his dreams, it gives me incentive to do the same." For his part, Maurice adds, "Hearing these Writes, learning about the cast of characters in Isabel's family (which is now my family!), I am constantly reminded and emboldened to go deeper into my own history."

Two people can love each other but not understand each other very well or even want the same things. When conflict arises between you, you can't relax until you resolve your differences or agree to live with them. Can you do Writes together if you have conflict? Perhaps, but it may not be easy. At the least it will take courage and restraint. You'll have to overhear your mate when he or she is in the process of formulating ideas and feelings that may sound threatening or insulting. To listen to your partner's Write while he or she is working something out can be upsetting or disturbing. Such disturbance may lead to resentment and defensiveness in either party, or it may enable you to think about each other and your situation in a new way. In the relative safety of a Write, you can listen to each other without having to do anything about what you hear. The powerful experience of overhearing someone thinking honestly about you can solidify the relationship if you are strong enough to take it in.

We know a couple whose twenty-year marriage was almost destroyed by revelations about the husband's affair with a family friend. Although he agreed to end the affair, tensions remained high. The wife, who had been practicing Proprioceptive Writing for many years, insisted that he begin practicing, too. Soon they began writing together, and found that they could listen to each other. Despite their anger and fear they were able, through their Writes, to calm down and reflect on the value of the marriage for each of them. They stopped being afraid it would fly apart if they heard the truth about what the other was feeling. They wrote to us saying: "We continue to write together. We are speaking with a candor we knew was possible and necessary, but which neither of us had dared to use before. Too bad we needed such a drastic lesson to force the issue, but then it takes whatever it takes."

Susan and Frank, both in their twenties, had been living together for two years when they began writing together. Unable to discuss their sexual dissatisfactions with each other, they decided to do a guided Write about sex. (She had not been orgasmic; he had not paid attention to foreplay.) This developed into a series of Writes in which eventually they described what they had never been able to say out loud: how they wished their partners to touch them. Both started by writing about their feelings, but soon, by describing their sexual fantasies in their Writes, they were able to give each other guidance. After several months of writing together regularly, Susan and Frank came for a workshop. Frank was beaming as Susan reported to us that she had finally had her first orgasm.

Parents Writing with Children

The American family of the twenty-first century is hard-pressed. With both parents working outside the home, and our speeded-up overscheduled lives, families get to spend less and less time together.

It seems clear to us that in the coming decades emotionally binding rituals such as Proprioceptive Writing will become increasingly necessary if family members want to stay in tune with one another. Once you have practiced it long enough to feel its benefits and be comfortable with it, but not before, you may want to do it with your children. We like to imagine the day when families, even those with very young children, regularly practice writing together and listen to one another thoughtfully, with an ear for the movement and strength of each individual member. We're not alone in this. People frequently come up to us after workshops asking for tips about doing Proprioceptive Writing with their kids. Let us describe how we did it in our family.

Even before Toby joined the family, three-year-old Francis, Linda's son, would play in the same room when Linda practiced Proprioceptive Writing. In the candlelight with the music playing, he built with blocks or drew, learning to concentrate on his activity as she concentrated on hers, two feet away, in that bubble of beautiful sound. In 1977, when Francis was four, Toby moved in and all three began to practice Proprioceptive Writing together.

Throughout his growing-up years, Francis was part of our family's Saturday night Proprioceptive Writing ritual, a sort of secular sabbath with activities we performed religiously. After dinner, we'd clear off the table and gather our drawing or writing materials. Phones were taken off the hook. We'd put on Baroque music or Hindu ragas and write or draw for about an hour. Occasionally, if he invited us to, we'd silently look over at what Francis was doing. When he was finished he would describe everything he'd just drawn, deepening and embellishing his thoughts as he went along. His comment on a drawing he made after a kidney operation when he was nine revealed his intense preoccupation. "If you could know what I know, about the liverest liver and the kidneyest kidney, you would flip." As he spoke knowingly of these hidden organs portrayed in the pulsating reds and blues of the drawing, we were struck by his confidence in his ideas and feelings.

If he was angry at something that happened, in school or in the playground or at home, he'd write it out:

What do I mean by Toby? *I mean that creep who got mad at me earlier for leaving my stuff in the hallway. I'd like to kick him in the butt. What do I mean by* kick?

Knock him to the moon so he could know what it feels like to be yelled at.

His tirade might go on a little longer, accompanied in this case by a line drawing of Toby sent soaring by a giant boot. When he was finished and asked himself the second question, he'd write some variation of this: "I'm not mad at Toby anymore. I feel hungry."

The spirit of those Saturday nights spent writing together permeated our everyday life, right through Francis's adolescence. For parents to allow children not only to feel emotions but to express them openly is among the most loving gifts they can offer. It takes patience to listen, and it's not always easy to hear what comes out. A parent's engaged but uncritical listening can strengthen a child's self-esteem, and through Proprioceptive Writing parents can teach their children values and skills that will serve and protect them for the rest of their lives. Above all, children can develop an interior life that they can enjoy without putting at risk the love and support of adults.

As with couples practicing Proprioceptive Writing together, there are some issues you'll have to consider before writing with your children. Can you concentrate on your own thoughts while practicing with your child? Can you be in his or her presence without making demands? How much decision-making power will you give your children? How much honesty can you bear to hear from your child? What if you overhear your child wondering about the allure of drugs or sex in a Write—will you use what is written to intervene? Or to snoop?

These are difficult and important questions, and only you and your children can answer them. But we can tell you from firsthand experience that if you do establish a Proprioceptive Writing practice, based on your own sense of what's right, you will feel more understanding of one another, enriched, and united as a family.

Afterword

Tommy, our haircutter, is still cutting hair in his nineties and was playing handball well into his eighties. Not only did he love the game but he beat other really good players at the local Y who were twenty years younger than he. One day Tommy told us how he did this: "You have to keep your eye on the ball," he said, as if it were his personal discovery. Then he added, with a chuckle, "People think it's easy to keep your eye on the ball, but it's not."

You are about to embark on a journey. Each time you have a Proprioceptive Write, you take a few steps on a path. You are heading in the right direction. Keep going. Keep your eye on the ball, though it's not always easy. That's all you really need to know.

How do you do this? By listening to what you write. Just as your eye must focus on the ball, your ear must focus on your words. Hearing gives rise to reactions and reflections. Write them. Get them down. Take as long as it takes to write your response. Then ask again. Listen. Don't be afraid of your emptiness. Hear what it says and write it.

But even if your thoughts run away from you—it's no easier to listen to yourself for twenty minutes than to keep your eye riveted to the ball—even if you're not sure if you're *hearing* your thoughts, your Proprioceptive Writing practice will grow.

Sonia, a retired theatrical agent, came from Arizona to Maine to do Proprioceptive Writing with us. She wrote every day, or twice a day, for two months and after that time her practice was firm. She wrote about the clients she had served, the marriages of her four children, her own marriage and divorce from a real estate magnate. She wrote about her immigrant mother and her adored father who died when Sonia was a child. She wrote about the ambitions of her youth, and her current projects. She loved her writing practice as an avenue for self-expression. She was so devoted to it that she even numbered her Writes and bound them in units of fifty.

One day, in the middle of her three-hundredth Write, Sonia had an epiphany. She began to hear herself as she never had before. She was writing her thoughts and feelings, as she always had, when something shifted in the way she listened to herself. For the first time she felt no investment whatsoever in what she was thinking. Never did she feel less pain about being who she was, never did she feel more herself.

A meditation master once said, if you wear the same clothes every day, eventually you'll begin to recognize yourself. If you practice Proprioceptive Writing every day, eventually you'll begin to hear yourself. Trust yourself, you're on the path. And remember the magic rules for self-trust: Write what you hear, listen to what you Write, and be ready to ask the Proprioceptive Question.

Notes

CHAPTER 1: *THE SOUND OF A VOICE THINKING*

Oliver Sacks, "The Disembodied Lady," in *The Man Who Mistook His Wife for a Hat* (New York: Summit Books, 1970), pp. 42–51.

Charles Olson, *Additional Prose* (Bolinas: Four Seasons Foundation, 1974), pp. 17–19.

David Bohm, *On Dialogue,* ed. Lee Nichol (Routledge: London and New York, 1988).

Walter J. Ong, *Orality and Literacy* (London: Methuen, 1982). See especially Chapter 4, "Writing Restructures Consciousness," pp. 78–116.

CHAPTER 2: *WRITE WHAT YOU HEAR: HOW THE METHOD WORKS*

Sheila Ostrander and Lynn Schroeder with Nancy Ostrander, *Superlearning* (New York: Delta/The Confucian Press, 1979). As Ostrander and Shroeder say, "the idea of music as the bridge to inner awareness goes back to the hidden sources of music itself." They report studies from eastern Europe in which students working to Baroque music experienced "expanded awareness and better memory" as well as various health benefits: "they felt refreshed, energized, centered. Tension and stress disappeared. Headaches and pains went. The impersonal physiological graphs printed out proof—lowered blood pressure, lowered muscle tension, slower pulse" (p. 81).

We find it suggestive that even plants tend to thrive when they're exposed to Baroque music for a while: "Plants grown in scientifically controlled chambers were given concerts of different kinds of music from rock to Baroque. Plants growing in the chambers given Baroque music by Bach and Indian music by Ravi Shankar rapidly grew lush and abundant with large roots. These plants leaned toward the music source 'so as to almost embrace the speaker.' Some leaned as much as sixty degrees. . . . Over the years as the same experiment with plants were repeated in universities and research centers, the same fact kept emerging—plants responded and grew abundantly, rapidly, and more healthfully when they were in a sonic environment of classical or Indian music compared with other kinds of music or silence" (p. 82).

In *Learn with the Classics* (San Francisco: The Lind Institute, 1999), authors Ole Andersen, Marcy Marsh, and Dr. Arthur Harvey conclude: "For the most part, there really is no other type of music that can do so much so well for your brain" (p. 44).

CHAPTER 3: *SELF-EXPRESSION: THE METHOD AS A PATH TO BETTER WRITING*

Ralph Keyes, *The Courage to Write* (New York: Henry Holt and Company, 1995), p. 3.

William James, *Psychology: The Briefer Course,* ed. Gordon Allport (Notre Dame, Ind.: University of Notre Dame Press, 1985), Chapter 2. Originally published in 1892 by Henry Holt and Company.

Schiller's letter is reproduced in many places. You can find it, along with interesting discussions, in Sigmund Freud's *The Interpretation of Dreams* (New York: Avon Books, 1965), p. 135, and in Zachary Leader's *Writer's Block* (Baltimore and London: The Johns Hopkins University Press, 1991), pp. 49–50.

"Horace: Five Epistles, translated from the Latin and with an Introduction by David Ferry," *The American Poetry Review* 30, no. 4 (July/August 2001): 23.

For the source of Alfred Kazin's comments, see his essay, "Jews," *The New Yorker,* March 7, 1994.

CHAPTER 4: *PROPRIOCEPTIVE INFORMATION: THE METHOD AS A PATH TO EMOTIONAL HEALTH*

James Pennebaker, "Writing about Emotional Experience Is a Therapeutic Process," *Psychological Science* 8 (1977): 162–166. Also see Pennebaker, *Opening Up: The Healing Power of Confiding in Others* (New York: Morrow, 1990).

A most dramatic suggestion for the far-reaching health benefits of emotional expression in writing was noted by Henry Massie, clinical associate professor of psychiatry at the University of California School of Medicine, in response to an article in *The New York Times* on what is known as the Nuns Study, begun in 1991. Studying the linguistic ability of ninety-three elderly Sisters of Notre Dame through autobiographical essays they submitted as part of their admissions procedures anywhere from fifty to seventy-five years earlier, researchers drew correlations between Alzheimer's disease and what they called "low idea density," or a lack of intellectual complexity in the youthful essays of the nuns who had developed the disease in later life. Of the two sample essays the *Times* reproduced, Massie observed an absence of the expression of emotion in the writing of the Sisters who died with Alzheimer's and five direct expressions of emotion and two metaphorical expressions of strong feeling in the writing by the Sisters who did not have the disease. In response to these observations Massie says, "It is possible that it is not merely cognitive complexity of thought at a young age that correlates with later health, but that having the ability to feel strongly and spontaneously helps organize and protect thinking as the years go by" ("Emotion May Have a Role in Alzheimer's," *The New York Times,* February 21, 1996).

Joshua Smyth, Ph.D., et al., "Effects of Writing about Stressful Experiences on Symptom Reduction in Patients with Asthma or Rheumatoid Arthritis: A Randomized Trial," *JAMA* 281 (April 14, 1999): 1304.

CHAPTER 5*: AWAKENING TO YOURSELF: THE METHOD AS A SECULAR SPIRITUAL PRACTICE*

D. T. Suzuki, *Zen and Japanese Culture* (Princeton, N.J.: Princeton University Press, 1970), p. 5.

Manfred Clynes, *Sentics: The Touch of the Emotions* (Garden City, N.Y.: Anchor Press/Doubleday, 1977), p. 218.

Suggestions for Further Reading

Here is a list of books about mind, meditation, writing, and related subjects that have stimulated our thinking about the proprioceptive method.

MIND

What's your idea of what a mind is? In *Maps of the Mind* (New York: Collier Books, 1981), author Charles Hampden-Turner diagrams and describes different concepts of mind as held by some of the world's most fascinating thinkers. Another of our favorites is Howard Gardner's *Frames of Mind* (New York: Basic Books, 1985). If you ever thought there was only one way to be smart, or that some forms of intelligence are superior to others, we hope you'll read this groundbreaking theory of multiple intelligences. It's a real eye-opener that will help put your own education into perspective.

The Dalai Lama has said that Buddhism is the study of mind. Books on meditation, spirituality, or religion can be wonderful everyday guides. Just reading them often feels enlightening. Some that we especially like are: Chögyam Trungpa's *Meditation in Action* (Boulder: Shambhala, 1969) and *Shambhala: The Sacred Path of the Warrior* (Boulder: Shambhala, 1984); Lawrence LeShan's *How to Meditate* (New York: Bantam Books, 1974); Bhagwan Shree Rajneesh's *Meditation: The Art of Ecstasy* (New York: Harper & Row, 1978); Tarthang Tulku's *Time, Space, and Knowledge* (Emeryville, Calif.: Dharma Publishing, 1977). Krishnamurti's approach to meditation through a vigorous inquiry into thought and thinking always gets our minds moving. See, for example, *Total Freedom: The Essential Krishnamurti* (San Francisco: HarperCollins, 1996).

William James's *The Varieties of Religious Experience* (New York: Penguin Books, 1982), originally published in 1902, is a classic in the field. His *Psychology, the Briefer Course* (published in 1892; edited by Gordon Allport and republished by Notre Dame, Ind.: University of Notre Dame Press, 1985) is to our mind the best introduction to psychology as well.

We find the concept of proprioception an enlightening way to understand consciousness. For this David Bohm's books are useful. They include: *The Proprioception of Thought* and *Thought as a System* (both published by David Bohm Seminars, P.O. Box 1452, Ojai, CA 93023) and, in collaboration with photographer Mark Edwards, *Changing Consciousness* (San

Francisco: HarperCollins, 1991), which urges a radical reexamination of the entire process of thought. See also books that transcribe conversations between Krishnamurti and Bohm.

Since, from one point of view, Proprioceptive Writing is about communication, you might be interested in looking at John Fiske's *Introduction to Communication Studies* (London: Routledge, 1990). If you'd like to dive into deeper waters, read anything by Gregory Bateson, considered by many to be one of the most original thinkers of the twentieth century. You might begin with Bateson's *Steps to an Ecology of Mind* (New York: Ballantine Books, 1972), then move on to *Angels Fear: Toward an Epistemology of the Sacred* (New York: Macmillan, 1987), a collaboration with his (and Margaret Mead's) anthropologist daughter, Mary Catherine Bateson, which explores the connection between mental processes and the biological world.

Read Joseph Chilton Pearce's *Evolution's End* (San Francisco: HarperCollins, 1992) to get a sense of the human potential for development in intelligence, creativity, and learning power, or read any of his other books. Pearce's commitment to teaching us how to nurture a child's potential is extraordinary in book after book.

LANGUAGE AND WRITING

In Chapter 3, we speak about the value of Proprioceptive Writing for writers. Any book about the writing process will undoubtedly enhance this discussion. See, for example, Annie Dillard, *The Writing Life* (New York: HarperPerennial, 1989); Brenda Ueland, *If You Want to Write* (St. Paul, Minn.: Greywolf

Press, 1987), originally published in 1938; Dorothea Brande, *Becoming a Writer,* with a foreword by John Gardner (New York: Tarcher/Putnam, 1981), originally published in 1934. You might also see *The Spirit of Writing,* edited by Mark Robert Waldman (New York: Tarcher/Putnam, 2001).

For works geared toward technique, see William Zinsser, *On Writing Well* (New York: HarperCollins, 2001). Also, Francis-Noel Thomas and Mark Turner, *Clear and Simple as the Truth* (Princeton, N.J.: Princeton University Press, 1994).

Though Proprioceptive Writing is not a literary form, it has elements in common with the personal essay and the memoir. *The Art of the Personal Essay,* edited by Phillip Lopate (New York: Anchor Books, 1994), is an anthology of personal essays, grouped historically and thematically, and a great read for anyone interested in the form. Lopate's now famous introductory essay to the collection is helpful. If you are interested in memoir writing or want to follow up on the discussion in Chapter 3 about "home movies" versus the "big screen," read Vivian Gornick's *The Situation and the Story* (New York: Farrar, Straus and Giroux, 2001).

Michael White and David Epston's *Narrative Means to Therapeutic Ends* (New York: W. W. Norton & Company, 1990) explores the relationship of writing to emotional health, the subject we took up in Chapter 4.

Inasmuch as Proprioceptive Writing is always about language, any study of language, from a literary to an anthropological point of view, may stimulate your thinking. For example see: Robin Lakoff's *Language and Woman's Place* (New York:

Harper & Row, 1975); George Lakoff and Mark Johnson's *Metaphors We Live By* (Chicago: University of Chicago Press, 1980); Steven Pinker's *The Language Instinct* (New York: William Morrow & Company, 1994); and David Abram's *The Spell of the Sensuous* (New York: Pantheon Books, 1996).

Most of these books are available in current paperback editions.

Suggestions for Music

The Baroque period is thought to begin in 1600 and end around 1750, the year of Johann Sebastian Bach's death. Along with George Frideric Handel and Antonio Vivaldi, Bach is considered the greatest of many wonderful Baroque composers. Others associated with the period include Albinoni, Palchabel, and Scarlatti. Every music store selling tapes and CDs should have an ample supply of Baroque music.

Relax with the Classics, the Lind Institute's four-volume collection of Baroque music, is a favorite of many Proprioceptive Writers. We have found all Lind Institute tapes and CDs to be of consistently high quality. For information, contact:

Lind Institute
P.O. Box 14487
San Francisco, CA 94114
Telephone: 1-800-462-3766
Website: www.lind-institute.com

Among Bach CD solo favorites for Proprioceptive Writers are Yo-Yo Ma's *6 Suites for Unaccompanied Cello* and John Williams's *Guitar Suites 1 & 3* and *The Four Lute Suites*.

As was mentioned in Chapter 2, we suggest you use Baroque for the first three months of your practice. After that, if you're inclined, experiment. You might enjoy Hindu ragas. Like Baroque, ragas have the steady rhythm and structural complexity that is thought to stimulate the whole brain. One collection that we have used for years is called simply *Ragas*, with Ravi Shankar and Ali Akbar Khan, although any tape or CD with Ravi Shankar would also work. Our students have also liked writing to *Evening Ragas from Benares* (Musical Heritage Society).

If you want to sample New Age music for study or learning, try the work of Steve Halpern, Brian Eno, Yanni, or Michael Jones. Some of our students also use the more avant-garde Eliane Radigue's *Kyema*.

If you are interested in reading about the way music affects your mind and increases learning powers, or the relationship between music and creativity, some books in this area are: Helen Bonny and Louis Savary's *Music and Your Mind* (New York:

Harper & Row, 1973); Sheila Ostrander and Lynn Schroeder's *Superlearning* (New York: Delta/The Confucian Press, 1979); Don Campbell's *The Mozart Effect* (New York: Avon Books, 1997); and Ole Andersen, Marcy Marsh, and Arthur Harvey's *Learn with the Classics* (San Francisco: The Lind Institute, 1999).

About the Authors

LINDA TRICHTER METCALF, PH.D., has been hailed as "a pioneering thinker in the field of writing." A native New Yorker, she graduated from the High School of Performing Arts in Manhattan and the City College of New York, and received her M.A. and Ph.D. degrees in literature from New York University. In the mid-1970s, as a professor at Pratt Institute searching for ways to help students find a writing voice, she created the practice now known as the Proprioceptive Writing method. Combining the art of literary criticism with therapeutic techniques, she has taught the method at such fine institutes as Esalen, Omega, and the New School University. In 1982, she and her partner, Tobin Simon, founded the Proprioceptive Writing Center in Maine, where they lived for many years, and, in

1996, they opened a new center in New York City, where she now lives, teaches individuals and groups, practices writing therapy, provides teacher-training in Proprioceptive Writing, and has recently launched a distance teaching program through the Proprioceptive Web site, www.Proprioceptivewriting.com.

TOBIN SIMON, PH.D., poet and educator, received his B.A. from Washington and Jefferson College, his M.A. from Stanford, and his Ph.D. from New York University. While a professor of English and Humanities at Pratt Institute, he began to collaborate with Linda Trichter Metcalf in 1977 in developing the Proprioceptive Writing method. He is cofounder and codirector of the Proprioceptive Writing Center, now in New York City, formerly in Maine. A poet and teacher of poetry for over forty years, he is expert at guiding students through the difficulties of the creative process and on to the satisfactions of completed work. A devoted coach, he has long used the Proprioceptive Writing method to teach poetry as well as to help men, individually and in groups, articulate their deepest feelings. Currently, he is at work on a book about step-parenting.

www.Proprioceptivewriting.com